DEATH

Meaning and Mortality
in Christian Thought
and Contemporary Culture

DEATH

Meaning and Mortality in Christian Thought and Contemporary Culture

MILTON McC. GATCH

The Seabury Press · New York

Grateful acknowledgment is made to Abingdon Press and to Professor Liston Mills for permission to use here, in expanded and revised form, Dr. Gatch's essay "Theological Reflection on Death from the Early Church to the Reformation," in *Perspectives on Death,* ed. Liston Mills (Nashville: Abingdon Press, 1969; copyright © 1969 by the publisher).

Library of Congress Catalog Number: 69-13541
627-169-C-4
Design by Nancy H. Dale
Printed in the United States of America

PREFACE

THIS BOOK WAS CONCEIVED and written as a whole, but I prefer to think of it in its completed form as four interrelated essays. The essay is often defined as an incomplete or exploratory discussion, and no analysis of this huge subject can more than scratch the surface of the kinds of materials available. As a student of medieval literature and thought, I have chosen to emphasize the place of death in Christian intellectual history. But even in Part II, I have constantly been aware of the selectivity and schematization of my approach.

As a medievalist, I have sometimes been inclined to think of this book as a sandwich in which Parts II and III were the meat and mayonnaise and Parts I and IV the bread. The former seem to me the substantive contributions to the whole. They emerged from my desire to set in a larger context my studies of the eschatology in Old English homiletic literature.

My only qualification for writing Parts I and IV is that I live in the times of which I write there. One of the first tasks of any medievalist is to be aware of the differences between the age he studies and that in which he lives. This awareness may give a perspective from which to speak of the present as well as the past. In Part IV, I have intentionally avoided the temptation to document my argument in order to underline the fact that the essay is not a learned argument but the personal reflection of a medievalist upon the present.

I avoided mentioning in those pages two very helpful books to which I should like now to direct my readers: Charles Hartshorne's *The Divine Relativity: A Social Conception of God* (New Haven: Yale University Press, 1948) and Norman

O. Brown's *Life Against Death: The Psychoanalytical Meaning of History* (Middletown, Conn.: Wesleyan University Press, 1959). I disagree with both in many important instances and could only have complicated this book by discussing either of them, but Hartshorne's analysis of the attributes of God as social concepts and Brown's assertion of the importance of the resurrection of the body influenced me greatly.

My debts are many. To mention only the most important, I should like to thank Professor Liston O. Mills, of Vanderbilt University, who commissioned the prototype of Part II as a lecture and allowed me to use again some of those materials; Arthur R. Buckley, of The Seabury Press, who made valuable suggestions about the kind of treatment of the subject which might be useful; and, among friends and colleagues who have helped me (without incurring culpability for faults which remain) to shape my thoughts and my prose, Professors Harvey H. Guthrie, Jr., Lloyd G. Patterson, Jesse P. Ritter, and William Williams.

I dislike the domestic acknowledgments which have become formulaic in the scholarly book, but I find myself obliged to enter two such notices. The first is to Lucinda, an eight-year-old guitarist and singer of protest songs, who was in agony for nine months because this book had no title and who contributed several typed lists of suggestions. I am sorry that I was not able to use *Death of the Days* or (because it is how I felt so often) *I CRY help Lord*. I am also happy to announce that my wife did not maintain our home as an island of quiet, free from the intrusions of the world, while I was writing this piece and that she hardly had time to read the manuscript, let alone to assist with the typing. She devoted herself instead to work for peace and justice; and, given the state of the world while I was working on this book, I might have lost faith in the whole project had she not been for me the figure of everything I was trying to say.

M. McC. G.

CONTENTS

PART I

Introduction

1 DEATH IN THE TWENTIETH CENTURY

IT IS ONE OF THE IRONIES of our century that we have experienced death by violence of sorts and on a scale heretofore unknown but that men in this century have not been able to discuss or to consider deeply the meaning of death.

Even the apparent exceptions to this observation tend to prove the rule. The First World War signified the demise of the Western Christian order and of an optimism born of a century of peace and progress. It, therefore, administered a profound shock, for thoughtful men were forced to reassess their view of the nature of man in the light of the depravity revealed by total war. The English poets of the war generation understood that the "Great War" was fratricidal and grotesque. Wilfred Owen, in particular, saw through the war to its sources in the nineteenth-century chauvinism and declared, reflecting on his encounters with the dead and dying on the battlefield, that the ancient sentiment of Virgil, "Dulce et decorum est pro patria mori" ("It is sweet and proper to die for one's country"), was "the old Lie." [1] The young soldier-poet paraphrased the story of the sacrifice of Isaac from Genesis to symbolize his understanding of current events in Europe. In Owen's version of the legend, however, Abraham does not stop the sacrifice of his son and substitute the "Ram of Pride" provided by the angel:

> But the old man would not so, but slew his son,
> And half the seed of Europe, one by one.[2]

Twentieth-century man, refusing to sacrifice his pride in order to maintain peace, had loosed upon himself, his progeny, and the nations a holocaust of death. (Benjamin Britten, in his *War Requiem,* written as a commentary on the Second World War to be performed at the opening of the new cathedral at Coventry, has doubled the poignancy of Owen's observation by setting it in juxtaposition with the lines of the Requiem offertory which speak of God's promise to Abraham and his seed that man would pass from death to life.) Owen is a poet of an age of mass death, but—like most of us in his age—he has nothing to say about the nature of death; he can only record a profound shock and dismay and, on occasion, venture to hope that out of the chaos will come a recognition of the fraternity of mankind which will help men to turn from the business of killing to the business of living.

Other poets of our century have been concerned with the problem of death as it is confronted by the individual. No such reflection is better known than the villanelle, "Do not go gentle into that good night," of Dylan Thomas in which one of the most frivolous and stilted French verse forms is made the vehicle for an urgent exhortation to the poet's dying father to struggle against death rather than face it with abject resignation.

> Do not go gentle into that good night.
> Rage, rage against the dying of the light.[3]

These two refrain lines urge the dying man to retain his will to live and continue the perennial battle of light against dark. Death, thus, is a symbol of that absurdity or futility which many poets and philosophers have considered the most salient characteristic of life in our century. It is a force against which the will of man must continually struggle. The meaning of death is again expressed in negative terms: it is "the dying of the light" and not a "good night."

In a sense, death must always be defined negatively, for it is the termination of biological life—the only mode of existence we know. Nevertheless, the twentieth century has had a curious reticence about discussing, defining, and even facing death. Death remains a great mystery for which twentieth-century man has had no satisfactory rationale, and of which he has had no explanation. The physical fact of death has been very much with us: the evening television news makes us participants in the slaughter of the battlefield and the highway as, urbanely, we sip our daily martini. We are continually warned that every cigarette brings us closer to death—and so forth. But we have not known the meaning of death. Because we have had no rationale of death, we have attempted to isolate ourselves from its manifestations.

Two recent books dealing with the social customs surrounding death in contemporary American and British society testify to the accuracy of this observation.

Jessica Mitford's *The American Way of Death* [4] is an exposé of the practices of the American "funeral industry" and an apology for the less expensive and less ostentatious programs of memorial societies. The book reveals much that must have been guessed by everyone who has attended an American funeral concerning the cost and (often unwanted) display which have become almost mandatory or which are, at least, irresistible to those who must, at a moment of extreme emotional stress, make a decision concerning the type of funeral a dead relative or friend is to be given.

In some ways, the most interesting aspects of the volume are its implications as to a general American consensus concerning the meaning of death. The phrase "the meaning of death" is perhaps the wrong one to use in this connection, however; for it is the self-appointed task of the funeral industry to "put on a well-oiled performance in which the concept of *death* [plays] no part whatsoever—unless it [is] inconsiderately mentioned by the clergyman. . . ." [5] In Miss Mitford's opinion, the funeral industry's chief goal (after making money) is to disguise the fact of death. Death is never mentioned; rather an elaborate vocabulary of euphemisms has been developed to circumvent the subject. And to go with the new language there is an array of furnishings and cosmetic techniques which completes or perfects the deception. Thus, when one's loved one passes on, he is elaborately groomed, finely dressed and "casketed." His casket, elegantly styled, lined, and mattressed, is designed to withstand the onslaughts of nature. After being displayed in a comfortable slumber room and eulogized in an ornate chapel, the loved one is transported by pastel Cadillac coach to be buried in a vault in an elaborate park at which the presence of an open grave is masked by a carpet of false grass and an embankment of flowers. If the loved one is cremated, his "cremains" are suitably enclosed and preserved. Even the expression "funeral service" has come to mean not the religious or other rites of memorial and burial but the service rendered by the "grief therapists," as undertakers like now to be called.

Miss Mitford rightly stresses the fact that contemporary American funeral customs are without historical precedent and mark a radical departure from the traditions of the nineteenth century.[6] She should, however, have taken account of the influence of urbanization and social mobility upon the prevailing burial fashions. Few persons now die at home in their own beds, as most did a century ago; and, even if they did, it would be nearly impossible in most contemporary societies for the families and friends of the dead to prepare bodies for burial and see them to the grave. It is precisely for this reason that those who wish to circumvent the funeral industry must form burial societies. As for social influences, it seems one must recognize that the manner of one's burial is as much a symbol of status as are the paraphernalia of his style of life. This is a fact which the industry perceives and exploits. But just as it is difficult to determine whether the blame for television programing is to be laid on the preferences of the public or the economic forces at work within a taste-forming industry, so it seems to many difficult to determine whether the public or the purveyor is to be blamed for undertakers' practices. Nevertheless, the case made in *The American Way of Death* is a potent one. Undertakers are to a remarkable degree taste-makers in matters funereal.

Perhaps in the case of contemporary funeral pomp, as with television programing, we ought to apply the maxim of Professor Marshall McLuhan, "The medium is the message." [7] The manner in which we bury the dead may, in other words, be more significant than what we say about death. If so, it must be concluded that Christian and non-Christian, religious or agnostic, Americans are agreed that death is taboo and must be disguised at all cost. The implication of Miss Mitford's evidence is that Americans believe the only way to face death is to hide it beneath needless, vulgar euphemisms and trappings which have been devised in an effort to deny the very existence of death. To put the very best face on the situation, we are afraid of the physical facts of death and its physical consequences and try to protect ourselves from these realities through an elaborate ritual conducted by a unique, neopriestly, pseudoscientific, and paramedical profession.

In the mind of that profession—and one suspects that the public does in general agree on this point—the new ritual surrounding death is soundly based on the "Judeo-Christian heritage" of our civilization. Miss Mitford, because of the limited purposes of her book, avoids this issue, although she is careful to marshal clerical support for her economic attack upon the funeral industry.[8] Historically, one of the implications of elaborate funeral customs and of preservation of the bodies of the dead has been belief in either immortality or reincarnation. And, similarly today, one can detect the strong implication both in the undertakers' statements and in public attitudes that somehow our traditional "Judeo-Christian" belief in immortality is being protected by the ritual of burial. Because life does not really end with death, we are more than willing to mask the temporary, but messy and discomforting, facts of physical death and decay. Or, to put the matter another way, because we are afraid to look too closely into the possibility of immortality (for fear that it may not be true), we are happy to enlist the services of the undertakers, whose task is to mask death so that disturbing questions need not arise.

This attitude was perceived and excellently satirized by Aldous Huxley in *After Many a Summer Dies the Swan*.[9] The central figure of the novel, Jo Stoyte, is a fabulous American tycoon, among whose many holdings is an elaborate cemetery at which erotic statuary and replicas of European monuments (a straightened tower of Pisa, the church of Stratford-upon-Avon) are so deployed as to take the mind off thoughts of death. But for Stoyte himself the deception that he works on others is not enough; for his cemetery "spoke to him of nothing but disease and death and corruption and final judgment. . . ." [10] Torn by memories of his religious heritage (a conglomerate of fundamentalism and Christian Science), he recites fervently at every moment of anxiety, "God is love. There is no death." [11] In Stoyte's entourage is his personal physician, Dr. Sigmund Obispo, who is at work on methods of lengthening life. Obispo and a scholar, who is indexing a collection of valuable papers acquired by Stoyte from an ancient English family, find that an eighteenth-century member of that family had discovered a method of rejuvenation and prolongation of life by means of ingesting the liver of carp. Indeed, Stoyte and his friends find that very man, the fifth Earl of Gonister, two hundred and one years old, living in the cellar of his manor house with a female companion. But the Earl is ugly, senile, apelike, subhuman. Nonetheless, Stoyte thinks the condition of that man preferable to death:

> Mr. Stoyte broke his silence, "How long do you figure it would take before a person went like that?" he said in a slow hesitating voice. "I mean, it wouldn't happen at once . . . there'd be a long time while a person . . . well, you know; while he wouldn't change any. And once you get over the first shock—well, they look like they were having a pretty good time. I mean in their own way, of course. Don't you think so, Obispo?" he insisted.[12]

The story of Jo Stoyte is based on the Greek legend of Tithonus, who was made immortal when he married a goddess. But the gift of immortality did not carry with it agelessness; and Tithonus, aged, became unacceptable to his wife, who shut him away. Huxley's title quotes a poem of Lord Tennyson on Tithonus in which the deified man is made to say that an endless life in which one must still age is horrible and to beg for restoration to that class "of happy men that have the power to die." [13] At the outset of the poem, Tithonus contrasts his lot with that of the mortals and longs for a life terminated by death:

> The woods decay, the woods decay and fall,
> The vapors weep their burthen to the ground,
> Man comes and tills the field and lies beneath,
> And after many a summer dies the swan.
> Me only cruel immortality
> Consumes; I wither slowly in thine arms,
> Here at the quiet limit of the world,
> A white-hair'd shadow roaming like a dream
> The ever-silent spaces of the East,
> Far-folded mists, and gleaming halls of morn.[14]

Unlike the Tithonus of myth, Huxley claims, the American Tithonus would rather risk an earthly immortality than face death, of which he is so afraid. Having confronted the horror of bestiality and senility in the self-made eighteenth-century Tithonus, Stoyte would still prefer to sacrifice his humanity than to face death. Stoyte, ironically, would never observe with tranquility that "after many a summer dies the swan."

What Miss Mitford observes in *The American Way of Death* may be evidence that we are a nation of Jo Stoytes. Death is abhorrent. We want to avoid the subject and to disguise the fact.

The situation in Britain as described by Geoffrey Gorer in *Death, Grief and Mourning* [15] differs in its outward manifestations but reveals similar fears and ambivalences. Mr. Gorer notes that between the First World War and the present the culturally imposed ritual of mourning has been virtually abandoned by Englishmen. Indeed, he believes that most Britons and Americans "tend to treat mourning as morbid self-indulgence, and to give social admiration to the bereaved who hide their grief so fully that no one would guess anything had happened." [16] His own experience has led him to believe that the absence of social forms of mourning has unfortunate psychological effects. The book is a report of the author's survey of the attitudes of a representative sample of recently bereaved Englishmen.

Whereas, in America, elaborate funerals have become the means for masking the realities of death, the British have moved in the last century in the direction of far simpler burial rites. [17] But the persons questioned in Gorer's sample display remarkable ambivalence and uncertainty as to how one is to explain death or to deal with it. Thus, for example, over one-third of those questioned stated that they said nothing to their children about the death of a relative; and nearly as many couched their explanations to children in religious euphemisms, though they themselves denied that they had religious convictions concerning death and afterlife. Children in agnostic families are, in other words, told that dead relatives have "gone to Jesus" or "gone to sleep," apparently because their parents have not themselves been able to integrate a concept of death within their own value structures.

A surprising number of those canvassed by Gorer believe in some form of afterlife.[18] Such an affirmation is evidently independent of religious affirmation or agnosticism. Only a very small percentage make a connection between afterlife and a doctrine of judgment, and none believe in eternal damnation. Rather, Britons tend to think of death as the beginning of a more pleasant mode of existence in which one may watch over those he has left behind. Not infrequently, the recently bereaved experience visions or dreams of those whom they mourn.[19] Gorer finds that the teachings of the churches have very little influence over the content of the beliefs of Britons concerning death.[20] Even those who claim a church affiliation seem to derive their notions from the general consensus of their society or from individual experience.

But the fear of mentioning death and of working through the grief syndrome in ways which are publicly evident, which apparently prevails in the United Kingdom, indicates that people are not certain of their beliefs about death. Mr. Gorer finds this so striking a situation that he has developed the hypothesis that, whereas frank treatment of sex has become socially acceptable in contemporary society, death has become a taboo subject in the drawing room and violent death the subject of a new class of pornographic literature and films.[21] The "pornographic" fascination with violent death in juxtaposition with the tendency to treat actual death in euphemistic and evasive terms is indicative of what Professor McLuhan, in the same connection, has called "a principle that the failure to face and evaluate unpleasant facts under conditions of art and controlled observation leads to a subsequent avalanche of the disagreeable." [22]

Neither Miss Jessica Mitford nor Mr. Geoffrey Gorer is concerned to analyze the content of our beliefs about death. The former is combatting the economic abuses of the funeral industry, and the latter is attempting to understand the impact of the abandonment of the rituals of mourning upon mourners. But both testify to the basic escapism of our attitudes toward death; and, ironically, there is also evidence in these books of the existence of a persistent belief in after-life, which the authors seem to take as a residual hangover from the Christian era.

The persistence of an idea of immortality of supposedly Christian origins among persons whose ideologies are not formed by the Christian churches can be explained in large part by reference to what has been called the "civil religion," which "actually exists, alongside of and rather clearly differentiated from the churches" and is "elaborate and well-institutionalized." [23] The teachings of the civil religion concerning the meaning of death as they were articulated at about the time of the Second World War have been admirably analyzed by W. Lloyd Warner in *The Family of God: A Symbolic Study of Christian Life in America.*[24] According to Warner, death removes the individual from historical or biographical time to a state of timelessness. The funeral rite marks, socially, a passage from the world of men and events to a "sacred realm where human and social time lose most of their meanings. . . . As opposites, dead and live time express the duality of existence, the sacred and the profane, the 'controlled' and the 'uncontrollable.' " [25] So it is that we place the dead in cemeteries and set them about with symbols of their new status: "The fundamental *sacred* problem of the graveyard is to provide suitable symbols to refer to and express man's hope of immortality through the sacred belief and ritual of Christianity, and to reduce his anxiety and fear about death as marking the obliteration of his personality—the end of life for himself and for those he loves." [26]

The cemetery functions as a part of the tacit social agreement that men "will not let each other die"; rationalistic dissenters from this agreement or faith proposition usually acquiesce to "the power of tradition and convention." [27] In terms of its social functions, it serves for the disposal of the corpse and to "provide a firm and fixed social place . . . where the disturbed sentiments of human beings about their loved dead can settle and find peace and certainty." [28] In its physical arrangements, both as regards the entire layout and the use of the separate lots, the graveyard tends to reflect the sociological structures of the living community. The family, the ethnic group, the fraternal organization, and military associations are almost as prominent in the symbolism of the "city of the dead" as are religious motifs. One sign of the upward mobility of a family may be the removal of the bodies of its forebears to a more socially respectable area of the burial grounds, or even to a more expensive cemetery. Such translations (as reinterments of the relics of saints used to be called) serve both to symbolize changes of status and to assuage the guilt feelings of the living toward the dead.

The cemetery represents the settled status of the dead. The transition from life to death is achieved by means of the funeral rites; and—like the other *rites de passage*: birth (baptism, circumcision), coming of age (confirmation, the twenty-first birthday), and marriage—such observances are tenacious. Even in a society undergoing rapid transformation, they are usually retained without significant change, for men need always to come to terms, ritually and liturgically, with these momentous changes of status. Thus (to cite only Warner's discussion of the Protestant activity):

The funeral oration must reassure the living that immortality is a fact, that the personality of the dead has not ceased to exist, and that spiritual life has no ending, since death is only the transition from life in the present to eternal life in a spiritual world. . . . The symbolic functions of the eulogy are to transform what are memories of the secular living into ideas of the sacred dead, and to re-form recollection of the personality sufficiently to make it possible for everyone to believe that entrance into heaven or any of its contemporary vague substitutes is not blocked or impossible.[29]

Warner's view of the undertakers as a professional group is similar to that of Miss Mitford but not so harsh, since he recognizes both their sociological functions and economic motivations as predictable and natural. The undertaker "is a private enterpriser who will do the ritually unclean and physically distasteful work of disposing of the dead in a manner satisfying to the living. . . ." [30] The practice of embalming provides an "informal" death mask which allows the living "to look at what they want to see in death": an image of temporary sleep. By means of his preparation of the body and managing the details of the rite, the undertaker "allows the living to pass through the phases of separation and margin with less pain than if he were not present." [31] Because of the uncleanness of his task, he is a natural "scapegoat." [32] Mr. Warner believes that as the church and its symbols become less and less important in the life of the community, the professional and parapriestly functions of the undertaker "will continue to grow." [33]

Such, in sociological and anthropological terms, is the general setting of American belief and practice concerning death. Lloyd Warner's analysis fills out Miss Mitford's with an interpretation of the ideological presuppositions of our mortuary customs. This is, however, only a preface to the author's discussion of the civic cult of the dead. It is his thesis "that the Memorial Day ceremonies, and subsidiary rites such as those of Armistice (or Veterans') Day, are rituals comprising a sacred symbol system which functions periodically to integrate the whole community with its conflicting symbols and its opposing, autonomous churches and associations." [34]

Cumulatively, the memorial rites communicate a sense "of triumph over death" and of a mutual solidarity closely akin to the feeling of unity which characterizes a nation during a war with whose aims the great majority of citizens agree. [35] The rites of Memorial Day—which begin with such events as Poppy Day and the observances of the several veterans' organizations and culminate with the oratory, parades and cemetery services of Memorial Day itself—are thematically unified. The most important motif is that of the sacrifice of the individual (whatever his social class or ethnic origin) for the general good. Lincoln is the prime example of purposeful sacrifice, and his Gettysburg Address is the sacred text for the occasion. The effect of the acts and oratory of the day is to emphasize that death can be a meaningful offering and that such death is not without its rewards, both in time and in eternity. The dead are held before the living as an example, and the living are urged to offer themselves as sacrifices for the ideals of the entire people. Inevitably, the rewards of sacrifice, described in terms of immortality, are stressed.

Warner's description of the civic religion's theology of death will strike a familiar chord with those who were reared in small cities or towns in America before or shortly after the Second World War. Its themes will also ring true for those who recall the state funeral and local expressions of mourning after the assassination of John F. Kennedy, whose own Inaugural Address is a masterful restatement of the basic theses of the civic religion.[36] Doubtless other nations have or have had civic cults of a similar sort, derived from but essentially independent of the teachings of the churches.[37]

One wonders, however, whether Warner's findings may not already be dated. Somehow John Kennedy's restatement seems to have been the last summary of the civic religious creed, already unimaginable in the cacophony of the latter half of his decade. Professor Robert Bellah speaks of a present "time of trial" for the civil religion in which "the problem of responsible action in a revolutionary world" [38] sorely tempts the national faith either to radical disbelief or to radical chauvinism. The answer, he believes, lies in a remolding of the vision in terms of international rather than local loyalties, of a new eschatology which would seek to share with all men the dreams of the old, national eschatology. One wonders, however, whether the vague theism of the civic religion may not itself collapse, just as the theism of the churches is threatened in a period of rapidly and radically changing forms of thought.

Whatever the case may be in this regard, it must be asked whether our basic assumptions concerning death remain unshaken. One senses under the language of books like those surveyed in this chapter an uneasiness which is inescapable but difficult to document because the subject is so difficult for men to treat.

Perhaps the matter can be expressed this way: we have lost our faith in the doctrine of immortality, but we know of no other way to deal with or to explain the phenomenon of death. For this reason, we attempt to mask death, to hedge it about so that it does not sorely threaten us if only because it has been made invisible. Not only do we attempt to avoid thinking of death, but also, in the absence of an acceptable rationale for the phenomenon, we find ourselves using the word pictures of conceptual systems to which we no longer adhere. Thus, to cite only one of the most striking examples, the daughter of Joseph Stalin describes the death agony of the self-professed atheist in the language of Eastern Orthodoxy. After his fatal stroke, she says, Stalin "was nothing but a body out of which the soul had flown"; and, later, "after a final effort, the spirit wrenched itself free of the flesh." [39] The startling incongruity of such statements rarely occasions comment. It is, somehow, an acceptable euphemism. Yet even in politically orthodox circles in Eastern Europe, circumlocutions for death are not uncommon. Arthur Koestler, in *Darkness at Noon,* has his protagonist, Rubashov, reflect as follows:

> In the Party death was no mystery, it had no romantic aspect. It was a logical consequence, a factor which one reckoned with and which bore rather an abstract character. Also death was rarely spoken of, and the word "execution" was hardly ever used; the customary expression was "physical liquidation." The words "physical liquidation" again evoked only one concrete idea: The cessation of political activity. The act of dying in itself was a technical detail, with no claim to interest; death as a factor in a logical equation had lost any intimate bodily feature.[40]

The framework which used to support our way of understanding and speaking of death has gone, and we lack both the terminology and the basic concepts for describing this universal event.

One of the most significant evidences of this situation is the very absence of a cogent contemporary literature treating philosophically or theologically of death. And yet the impression remains strong among many who do not claim allegiance to Christianity that belief in immortality is a foundation stone of the Christian creed. Gorer, for example, remarks that "the reason why the Christian clergy are so continuously involved in the disposal of the dead is that orthodox Christianity is dogmatic that the soul continues to exist after death."[41] He seems to believe that although many still turn to the church to assist in the disposal of the dead, Britons cannot face open expression of grief because they have no value system to undergird such practices. But let someone suggest that immortality is not a doctrine essential to the Christian tradition, and the outcry is immediate and anguished. Professor Oscar Cullmann discovered this when he published a lecture in which he asserted that the notion of immortality was, in fact, alien to the early church.[42] Warner (whose evidence was gathered in the 1930's, checked against the attitudes of the 1940's and published in the 1950's) cites the Memorial Day oration of a member of a fraternal group:

> Savant and savage are equally dumb before the question: If a man die, shall he live again? No traveller has ever returned with maps or field notes of a life beyond the grave. The marvelous thing about it is that, despite the fact, all of us or almost all of us believe in the life hereafter. It is the universal belief of mankind, a belief that never had to be taught us, we just naturally believe it.[43]

Everyone has heard that sort of statement. There is evidence in our funeral customs that we want very much to believe something of the sort but that we find it difficult to do so. Few of us would argue against the point, especially in the presence of the mourning; but it is surprising that the taboos are so strong that few care to discuss the issue of death and the afterlife openly.

The word "afterlife" has not figured prominently in this discussion, but it has been implicit throughout. The concepts of afterlife and immortality, closely related and apparently of great antiquity, seem almost implicitly to motivate our contemporary funeral customs which are designed to perpetuate our belief that personality is not obliterated by physical death. But our funerals and civic rites are also contrived in such a way as to avoid raising embarrassing questions about the future of man for fear that the answer might have to be that death is the end of man's existence.

At least in part, the situation arises from the fact that Christians and non-Christians alike in Western culture have assumed that a doctrine of immortality and a promise of an afterlife are, together, the foundation and chief sanction of Christian belief. It is the purpose of what follows to suggest that this proposition is, at the very least, historically dubious and to consider new approaches to the problem of death which might lead us away from the present unhealthy impasse.

Part II, the first of the three essays which follow, analyzes key statements concerning death from ancient Greece and the Bible through the early-seventeenth century in an effort to show what have been the basic Christian attitudes toward death and the afterlife. In Part III some problems of interpreting these documents are considered, and, finally, an effort (with help from three significant pieces of modern fiction) is made to reformulate a Christian view of death in the light of contemporary patterns of thought and of the historical tradition.

PART II

Immortality and Resurrection: A Sampling of the Intellectual Traditions

1 THE GREEK TRADITIONS

THE CHRISTIAN INTELLECTUAL heritage is an offspring of the marriage performed by the church Fathers of two traditions: the Greek tradition as it had descended to Hellenistic culture and the Hebraic tradition mediated by the primitive Christians. Any retrospective effort to separate these two sources is difficult; indeed, the extent to which the mingling of Greek with Hebrew thought had proceeded by the time of the rise of Christianity is only now being recognized. Nevertheless, it is necessary to attempt an analysis of the kinds of sources from which Christian views concerning death and the subsequent destiny of man arose. In their attitudes toward death and man's destiny after death, the Greek and the Hebrew were strikingly different.

For the Greek background, no two figures are more suitably or more clearly contrasted than Thucydides and Plato, both of whom wrote at about the beginning of the fourth century B.C., and both of whom were profoundly affected by the events of the fifth century, during which Athens at first rose to the apex of imperial power and later suffered disabling defeat in the Peloponnesian War.

THUCYDIDES AND CIVIC IMMORTALITY

In the History of the Peloponnesian War, Thucydides reports an oration or eulogy which Pericles, the leader of the Athenian democracy, purportedly delivered at the public funeral for the soldiers who had died in the first engagements of the war. Primarily concerned with civic virtues,[1] the Funeral Oration is nevertheless revealing as to one facet of the approach of the Greek intellect to the problem of death. It reads in part:

. . . Many are the proofs which we have given of our power and assuredly it does not lack witnesses, and therefore we shall be the wonder not only of the men of to-day but of after times; we shall need no Homer to sing our praise nor any other poet whose verses may perhaps delight for the moment but whose presentation of the facts will be discredited by the truth. Nay, we have compelled every sea and every land to grant access to our daring, and have everywhere planted everlasting memorials both of evil to foes and of good to friends. Such, then, is the city for which these men nobly fought and died, deeming it their duty not to let her be taken from them; and it is fitting that every man who is left behind should suffer willingly for her sake.

It is for this reason that I have dwelt upon the greatness of our city; for I have desired to show you that we are contending for a higher prize than those who do not enjoy such privileges in like degree, and at the same time to let the praise of these men in whose honour I am now speaking be made manifest by proofs. Indeed, the greatest part of their praise has already been spoken; for when I lauded the city, that was but the praise wherewith the brave deeds of these men and men like them have already adorned her; and there are not many Hellenes whose fame would be found, like theirs, evenly balanced with their deeds. And it seems to me that such a death as these men died, gives proof enough of manly courage, whether as first revealing it or as affording its final confirmation. And, even in the case of those who in other ways fell short of goodness, it is but right that the valour with which they fought for their country should be set before all else; for they have blotted out evil with good and have bestowed a greater benefit by their service to the state than they have done harm by their private lives. And no one of these men either so set his heart upon the continued enjoyment of wealth as to become a coward, or put off the dreadful day, yielding to the hope which poverty inspires, that if he could but escape it he might yet become rich; but, deeming the punishment of the foe to be more desirable than these things, and at the same time regarding such a hazard as the most glorious of all, they chose, accepting the hazard, to be avenged upon the enemy and to relinquish these other things, trusting to hope the still obscure possibilities of success, but in action, as to the issue that was before their eyes, confidently relying upon themselves. And then when the moment of combat came, thinking it better to defend themselves and suffer death rather than to yield and save their lives, they fled, indeed, from the shameful word of dishonour, but with life and limb stood stoutly to their task, and in the brief instant ordained by fate, at the crowning moment not of fear but of glory, they passed away.

And so these men then bore themselves after a manner that befits our city; but you who survive, though you may pray that it be with less hazard, should resolve that you will have a spirit to meet the foe which is no whit less courageous. . . .[2]

The purpose of Thucydides in putting these words into the mouth of the great leader of fifth-century Athenian democracy was to give a picture of the ideals upon which the achievement of Athens was based at the outset of the events which led to the corruption and destruction of the democratic empire.[3] It begins with a description in broad terms of the glories of Athenian democracy, implicitly contrasted against Spartan practice, and proceeds to an evaluation of the sacrifices of those who died in the first engagements of the Peloponnesian War.

To understand Thucydides' and Pericles' point of view, it is necessary, first, to appreciate the Greek view of the nature of the individual's relationship to the *polis,* or city-state. In the modern West, the individual is usually conceived as an almost autonomous and basic unit. Thus, one allies himself freely with the state, which achieves its glory through the dedication of such noble-minded, free individuals. From the ancient Greek point of view, such an understanding was incomprehensible. The city, which derived from the family or tribe and was thought to be a family-like institution, defined the existence of the individual. One's whole destiny depended upon the social unit in which fortune had placed him, and his achievements were judged as they contributed to or detracted from the well-being and fame of the city or family in which he had his existence. The role of the citizens as the chorus in the Greek drama is closely related to this view of things, and the hero acts out his role against the background of his city. Frequently his tragedy arises from or results in his alienation from the city. In *Oedipus Rex,* for example, Oedipus vows at the outset to do whatever is necessary to rid his city of the plague. Both the irony and the tragedy of the play result from the fact that the king himself is the cause of the sacrifice of those who fell in war can only be defined by the gods. Although the taboos against incest and patricide are clearly important in the play, it is a modern fault to see the tragedy of Oedipus as located in the violation of these prohibitions. Oedipus' tragedy was, at base, that to fulfill his duty as king by purging the city of its disaster he had to destroy himself. His being and duty were defined by the city.

So it is that Pericles begins with an allusion to the founding fathers and passes to an attempt to define the genius of Athens.[4] Its constitution is distinguished by its democracy, which allows the citizen an unprecedented freedom and opportunities for intellectual refinement without loss of manliness. Its society is an open one in which civic duty includes contribution to the effort of defense. Athens has become "the school of Hellas," the exemplary city with the mission of maintaining its tradition in order to lead others to similar enlightenment and well-being.

Only in this context can one evaluate the meaning of those deaths to which the Oration in Thucydides' *History* serves as an epitaph.[5] In the passage quoted above, Pericles asserts that the lives and deaths of her citizens themselves are sufficient advertisement for the glory of the city. The services of no epic poet are needed, because the facts of the Athenian achievement require no poetic embellishment. The greatness of the sacrifice of those who fell in war can only be defined and appreciated in the light of the greatness of the city itself.

Praise of the city is, indeed, praise of the dead men. In this light and in that of their deaths, the quality of their lives before the final battle becomes irrelevant. The important thing is that, at the crucial moment, they chose to stand for the city and to flee "from the shameful word of dishonor." The city is, therefore, their memorial, and they are its example.

> For the whole world is the sepulchre of famous men, and it is not the epitaph upon monuments set up in their own land that alone commemorates them, but also in lands not their own there abides in each breast an unwritten memorial of them, planted in the heart rather than graven on stone.[6]

In this faith, the mourning are to find consolation, and those who are young enough are to have courage to persevere and to continue to propagate the city.

Thucydides gives Pericles no explicit reference to immortality, but the implication is clear that sacrifice for the state gives a kind of deathlessness by contributing to the fame of the city, to its role as "the school of Hellas." More explicit is the thought of Tyrtaeus, the seventh-century B.C. poet of Sparta, who describes the glory of the death of the devoted soldier in battle:

His glory or his name shall never die,
   Though 'neath the ground, he deathless shall remain,
Whom fighting steadfastly, with courage high,
   For country and for children Mars has slain.

But if he 'scape the fate of death's long sleep,
   And bear victorious conquest's bright renown,
Then young and old shall him in honour keep,
   Till full of joys he to the shade sink down.[7]

Greek man, who understood himself primarily as citizen, believed that fame for his valor as a citizen granted a kind of immortality, or at least a survival for his name. In a sense, this is a metaphoric immortality, since it does not speak of continued existence for the person; yet, given the importance of the social unit as the structure in terms of which the individual derived his understanding of selfhood, it is something more than a metaphor: "for it assures man of the imperishable value of his personality, which is invested in his name and fame." [8]

The reverse possibility, a negative judgment of a man's life and actions, is also understood in this strand of Greek thought. On another occasion, faced with grumblings among the citizens because of hardships endured during a plague and contemporaneous setbacks in the war efforts against the Spartans, Pericles distinguished between the results of military undertakings, for which men are responsible, and of natural disaster, for which men are not culpable. He could, thus, develop the negative implication of the Funeral Oration—dishonorable action may lead to the eternal obliteration of one's name instead of its immortality in the memory of the city. "Do you, then," he urged the assembly, "providently resolving that yours shall be honour in ages to come and no dishonour in the present, achieve both by prompt and zealous effort." [9]

If, in their political contexts, such teachings seem today to have chauvinistic overtones, they have also the merit of being logically derived from the Greek definition of man as a being who lives in a *polis* [10] and understands himself above all as a member of the city. The roots of the doctrine of immortality lie not in a doctrine of the soul but in an understanding of the social nature of man.

PLATO AND PERSONAL IMMORTALITY

In 399 B.C., the philosopher Socrates was condemned to death by the Athenian *polis* for corrupting the youth of the city by his teaching and for atheism. His final conversation with his disciples was recorded by Plato in a dialogue in which Phaedo, one of the followers of Socrates, recounts the events of the last day in the life of the master for other friends who had not been present. Not surprisingly, the conversation turned upon the meaning of death:

> Of course [Socrates remarks] you know that when a person dies, although it is natural for the visible and physical part of him, which lies here in the visible world and which we call his corpse, to decay and fall to pieces and be dissipated, none of this happens to it immediately. It remains as it was for quite a long time, even if death takes place when the body is well nourished and in the warm season. Indeed, when the body is dried and embalmed, as in Egypt, it remains almost intact for an incredible time, and even if the rest of the body decays, some parts of it—the bones and sinews and anything else like them—are practically everlasting. That is so, is it not?
>
> Yes.
>
> But the soul, the invisible part, which goes away to a place that is, like itself, glorious, pure, and invisible—the true Hades or unseen world—into the presence of the good and wise God, where, if God so wills, my soul must shortly go—will it, if its very nature

is such as I have described, be dispersed and destroyed at the moment of its release from the body, as is the popular view? Far from it, my dear Simmias and Cebes. The truth is much more like this. If at its release the soul is pure and carries with it no contamination of the body, because it has never willingly associated with it in life, but has shunned it and kept itself separate as its regular practice—in other words, if it has pursued philosophy in the right way and really practiced how to face death easily —this is what "practicing death" means, isn't it?

Most decidedly.

Very well, if this is its condition, then it departs to that place which is, like itself, invisible, divine, immortal, and wise, where, on its arrival, happiness awaits it, and release from uncertainty and folly, from fears and uncontrolled desires, and all other human evils, and where, as they say of the initiates in the Mysteries, it really spends the rest of time with God. Shall we adopt this view, Cebes, or some other?

This one, by all means, said Cebes.

But, I suppose, if at the time of its release the soul is tainted and impure, because it has always associated with the body and cared for it and loved it, and has been so beguiled by the body and its passions and pleasures that nothing seems real to it but those physical things which can be touched and seen and eaten and drunk and used for sexual enjoyment, and if it is accustomed to hate and fear and avoid what is invisible and hidden from our eyes, but intelligible and comprehensible by philosophy—if the soul is in this state, do you think that it will escape independent and uncontaminated?

That would be quite impossible, he said.

On the contrary, it will, I imagine, be permeated by the corporeal, which fellowship and intercourse with the body will have ingrained in its very nature through constant association and long practice.

Certainly.

And we must suppose, my dear fellow, that the corporeal is heavy, oppressive, earthly, and visible. So the soul which is tainted by its presence is weighed down and dragged back into the visible world, through fear, as they say, of Hades or the invisible, and hovers about tombs and graveyards. The shadowy apparitions which have actually been seen there are the ghosts of those souls which have not got clear away, but still retain some portion of the visible, which is why they can be seen.

That seems likely enough, Socrates.

Yes, it does, Cebes. Of course these are not the souls of the good, but of the wicked, and they are compelled to wander about these places as a punishment for their bad conduct in the past. They continue wandering until at last, through craving for the corporeal, which unceasingly pursues them, they are imprisoned once more in a body. And as you might expect, they are attached to the same sort of character or nature which they have developed during life.[11]

The passage quoted is not necessarily the most central to the argument of the *Phaedo;* but it has been of immense importance for the history of thought, and its elucidation must take account of most of the crucial passages of the dialogue and of the doctrine of recollection, which is at the heart of the Platonic notion of the soul.

The *Phaedo,* like many of Plato's Socratic dialogues, is carefully devised so that the author is not committed to the views expressed. Plato was unable to be present the day Socrates died, and Phaedo is made to report the last conversation of the great philosopher. Furthermore, it will be seen below that Socrates himself was evidently very careful not to commit himself to the mythological examples he used to illustrate his argument. Thus, it is as difficult as it is vital to define exactly the nature of Plato's beliefs.[12]

After Zanthippe, the wife of Socrates, has been led away weeping, one of those present asks the doomed man why he has been writing poetry of late and is told that he does so in response to a vision. Next, the philosopher is asked why he has cautioned in his teaching against suicide. The reply is that, although a philosopher must always be willing to die, man is the keeper of his life for the gods and must leave the question of the termination of life to the gods. The disciples, however, are not satisfied with this response; and the dialogue turns to a full-dress discussion of how it is "natural that a man who has really devoted his life to philosophy should be cheerful in the face of death, and confident of finding the greatest blessing in the next world when his life is finished." [13]

Socrates' definition of death assumes at once the existence of two separable entities, one of which can exist independently of the other. Death is "simply the release of the soul from the body." [14] This dualism of the physical and the incorporeal is absolutely vital to what follows, for in Socrates' view the body is a hindrance to the soul as it seeks to acquire knowledge. Truth, like the soul is incorporeal; there exist absolutes or ideas of goodness, beauty, and the like, understanding of which by the soul is impeded by the physical distractions and desires of the body. Thus, "if we are ever to have pure knowledge of anything, we must get rid of the body and contemplate things by themselves with the soul itself." [15] True and full knowledge is impossible so long as the soul is joined to the body. Death, therefore, is a happy event, a moment of fulfillment for the seeker after truth. The notion of "freeing" [16] the soul from the body must be added to that of "separation."

At this point in the discussion, Socrates turns to the "allegorical meaning" [17] of the initiatory rites of the mystery cults, in which the notions of purgation and purification played a decisive role, for an example: the life of philosophy is a kind of purgative and purificatory discipline by which one prepares the soul for what is to come.

The disciples are now satisfied that the philosopher must face death with equanimity because of the nature of the soul. But now they must ask about the soul's fate after its freedom from the body has been gained. Might it not, as some philosophers had suggested, simply "be dissipated like breath or smoke, and vanish away"? [18] The answer to this problem is long and difficult. It involves, at first, the concepts of reincarnation and of the generation of all things from their opposites. Since death comes from life, it is reasonable to assume that there is a cosmic rhythm whereby pre-existent souls enter bodies at birth, pass from them at death and, after some time, enter bodies again to renew the cycle.

The core of the argument, however, is based on the crucial Socratic teaching "that what we call learning is really just recollection." [19] Knowledge, according to Plato's Socrates, seems not to be the inculcation of truths but the recollection of truths formerly known to the soul and evoked by putting the right kinds of questions to the body-bound intelligence. This epistemological and educational doctrine presupposes that the soul which recalls truths knew those same truths in a previous existence, one in which it may have experienced truth at first hand. Truth, in this sort of argument, must be regarded as "absolute reality," [20] eternal and unchanging. The state of wisdom, which is an engagement of this ultimate, must therefore be a condition in which the soul, for the time, frees itself from the mutability and distinctiveness of the body.

It is in this context that the passage quoted at the head of this discussion belongs. The soul, after it is separated from the body, enters into an existence which depends for its quality upon the nature of its life with the body, upon the degree of its contamination or emancipation by means of wisdom. One conceives of degrees of existence, ranging from pure incorporeality—a life "as they say of the initiates in the Mysteries . . . with God" [21]—to the state of such shadowy apparitions as ghosts.

Philosophy is to be understood as an exercise in recollection, an effort to free the soul from the corporeal. The philosopher, in a sense, does during his life what death does for the soul. Therefore, the philosopher need never fear death, which is only the culmination of his life work.

Socrates deals next with two objections to the notions he has expounded. The first is that of the Pythagoreans, that the soul is to be conceived, as is attunement in musical theory, as a principle which holds the body in balance but which cannot exist independent of its relationship to the body. The doctrine of recollection answers this theory; for the soul must be both immortal and imperishable, since it can be taught to recall its experience of the ideal and absolute. Second, it is suggested, without contradicting the doctrine of recollection or the idea of regeneration, that the soul may be only relatively long-lived but not truly immortal. The answer to this argument is based on Socrates' belief that absolute, ideal forms exist and that from our recollection of these we derive our knowledge. The ideal forms, in other words, are causative. Since the presence of soul is necessary to give the body life, and because the idea of life does not admit of its opposite, death, the soul must be immortal.

"If the soul is immortal, it demands our care not only for that part of time which we call life, but for all time," [22] Socrates remarks, turning to a concluding section on one's duties toward his soul. He illustrates his point by referring to the myth of the guardian angel, which guides the separated soul on its journey to suitable reward or punishments and speculates at length on the nature of the cosmos and the places in which souls may ultimately dwell. But at the end he cautions against literal acceptance of such illustrative speculations. The important thing is that the soul is immortal. On this belief, he is confident and even triumphant as his own death approaches. So Socrates ends the discussion and prepares to bathe before drinking the poison which has been prepared for him.

Plato has put into the mouth of Socrates a remarkable and evasive body of teachings. Anyone who is the least familiar with standard or traditional Christian world-pictures will have recognized immediately that the passage quoted at length above is clearly a chief source for what was to become the Christian mythic picture. But the outline of the *Phaedo* ought to make it as clear that Plato has been careful not to commit himself to these mythic details. They are illustrative of his faith. Poetic and active, they simply dramatize the implications of belief in the existence of absolutes and of the doctrine that all learning is but recollection by the immortal part of man of what he has known before.

Between Plato and the church Fathers there was a long and important tradition of philosophical investigation which tended not only to affirm what Plato had taught but also to literalize and to systematize his contributions. All the disarming tentativeness of the discourse of Socrates in the dialogues was lost on the way. In the original, the myth of the journey and rewards of the soul was a pictographic effort to clarify notions which were difficult to grasp because they were so abstract. That the soul was imperishable was a necessary deduction from the basic hypothesis that learning is recollection. This alone was enough to allow Socrates to drink the cup of hemlock with more than an air of self-possession and equanimity. The state simply gave him an opportunity to vindicate in his own eyes his basic heresy: the teaching that by free (and often apparently seditious) inquiry one might recall the truth.

Allusion to the role of the state in this connection is no mere accident, for it has sometimes been suggested that the collapse of Athens and its ideals, which was chronicled by Thucydides, made inevitable the shift from emphasis on the political or social immortality hinted at by Pericles to the personal immortality of Socrates. His social order in disarray, man had to fall back upon his own inner strengths and resources, to examine his claims to personal uniqueness and dignity.[23]

Plato's most extended discussion of the relationship of politics, ethics, and philosophy, the *Republic,* concludes with a narration of the experiences of a soldier who, having died in battle, later revived to recount his experiences in the other world.[24] In this account, it is abundantly clear that Plato's doctrine of immortality is also a paradigm for the teaching of civic morality. The essential contrast with the kind of immortality implied by Thucydides is that this immortality is not won from one's fellow citizens but that it is earned "from God." [25] This fusion of the civic theme with the epistemological doctrine of recollection had a decisive influence upon the Roman moralist, Cicero, whose own *Republic* ends, after the example of Plato's, with a dream-vision, in which Scipio sees the rewards of good citizenship as a blissful future existence for the soul.

The two Greek views surveyed in this chapter stand in stark contrast. For the one, immortality is a gift of men to a man who has served his society well. It resides in the collective memory of the *polis*. For the other, immortality is of the nature of man and the cosmos; and yet the idea of immortality is simply a logical consequence of the basic tenet that truth is absolute. To put it another way, for Thucydides immortality is extrinsic to one's humanity. It is the reward of the city to a man whose deeds are worthy of being remembered. In this respect, Thucydides' position is analogous to that of the twentieth-century civic religion which was discussed in the first part of this book. In the writings of Plato, however, immortality is intrinsic in the very concept of man and of the human quest for knowledge. One has, at the outset, two conflicting traditions. Both emphasize the importance of the quality of a man's life in his society in determining his destiny. But, for the former, that destiny may be the immortality of his memory, and, for the latter, it is the immortality of his soul.

2 THE BIBLICAL TRADITION

ON THE WHOLE, it can be said of the biblical writings that they have no theology of death or of an afterlife. Both Testaments are radically secular in their overriding concern with history, which is to be understood in both in a very special sense as the self-manifestation of God in human events or as the interpretation and judgment of human events in the light of man's highest aspirations—which the Hebraic tradition viewed as the will of God for men.[1] Concerned with the destiny of a People in history, the writers of Scripture had little to say about the significance of the end of the individual's historical existence and were not motivated to speculate about an extrahistorical survival. Passages which seem to belie this generalization must be read very carefully within the special historical circumstances which gave rise to them. Any effort to understand the biblical view of the nature of death and man's destiny must, in other words, keep constantly in mind the resounding silence of the Bible on the subject in general and be tempered by a very careful interpretation of its few specific statements within their historical contexts.

THE OLD TESTAMENT

The Old Testament records the historical and theological reflections of a People for over a millennium, during which time considerable development and alteration of ideas are observable. Despite their wide divergencies of points of view, nevertheless, the Hebrew writers uniformly approached the question of death in a manner quite different from those of either the Greeks or the moderns.[2]

The prevailing opinion concerning death can be expressed in two ways. One might say either that death was regarded as the termination of human existence or that, because the predominant concern was with the People and its historical destiny, the question of the significance of death for the individual rarely arose and was essentially meaningless. From the point of view of the modern world, which is uniquely concerned with the role and identity of the individual, the former restatement of the biblical approach to death is probably the more congenial; historically, the latter is surely the more accurate.

The concerns of the dying patriarch, Abraham, as related in the Yahwist history, touch upon several of the chief themes in the basic biblical understanding of death:

> Abraham was now old, advanced in years; and Yahweh had blessed Abraham in everything.
>
> Abraham said to the senior servant of his household, who had charge of all his possessions, "Place your hand under my thigh, and I will make you swear by Yahweh, God of heaven and God of the earth, that you will not obtain a wife for my son from the daughters of the Canaanites among whom I dwell, but will go to the land of my birth to get a wife for my son Isaac. . . . On no account are you to take my son back there! Yahweh God of heaven, who took me from the home of my father and the land of my birth, and who solemnly promised me, saying, 'I will give this land to your offspring'—he will send his angel before you that you may bring my son a wife from there. . . ." So the servant placed his hand under the thigh of his master Abraham and swore to him concerning this matter. (Gen. 24:1-9) [3]

This account of the death of Abraham is a passage from the Yahwist epic of the history of the Hebrew peoples. The writer of this great narrative was concerned to set out the historical framework within which the present state of the kingdom of Judah was to be understood. He believed that by telling of the nomadic patriarchs, the tribal confederacy, and the emergence of the Davidic kingship, he could explain how it had come to pass that a tribal people had prospered among the other peoples of the ancient Near East, whose cultures and religions contrasted markedly with those of the worshipers of Yahweh. For the Yahwist historian, in other words, history supplanted myth as the means of explaining the meaning of the experience of the People.[4] The account of the life of Abraham holds a pivotal place among the earlier chapters of this epic of the People's history, and the treatment of the death of the patriarch typifies the essential concerns of earlier Hebraic thought in dealing with the termination of life.

At the end of his full and prosperous life, Abraham remembered that one task remained unfinished. He had not provided for the continuation of his line beyond the next generation. Thus, his dying act[5] was to cover this oversight. One can hardly say that he was motivated to this ultimate intervention in Isaac's affairs, after the manner of the dying patriarch of the modern novel, either by a generous desire to see that his son would be cared for when the father was no longer there to oversee his activities or by a malicious compulsion to continue his parental tyranny even in death. Rather, he wanted to see that the achievements of his lifetime would be continued; and this could only be done through Isaac and his progeny.

Abraham believed that he had come to live among the Canaanites through the intervention of Yahweh and that this settlement was not a matter of a generation or two but a permanent one. The Yahwist historian stresses this conviction again and again, but chiefly by means of the quotation of the promise of the "God of heaven and God of the earth." The promise is stated not in terms of Abraham himself but in terms of his "offspring." In other words, the Patriarch conceives of the meaning of his life not in terms of his own accomplishments but in terms of the fulfillment of the promise he had received. He is not to be regarded as a remarkable man of unusual and significant achievements but as an actor in the continuing processes of purposeful historical development. He will remain important only insofar as what he has begun in his lifetime is continued in the history of his offspring. He will assume a place in the genealogies of his people and will remain a vital link in the chain which is being forged in the history of the People. The unusual oath which Abraham makes the servant swear upon his genitals probably underlines this general point of view.[6] In those who proceed from his thighs, both his life and his death assume significance.

There is no attempt (indeed, it is not possible) to speak in individual terms of Abraham, for the Hebraic mind does not conceive of the situation as we do. There is no way to separate Abraham from the clan he produces. Even his personality is indistinct from that of the tribe. Thus, one can only speak anachronistically of his death as an end since, even dead, Abraham continues to be an important aspect of the corporate personality. Such was also the meaning of the priestly historian who, in his account of the death of the Patriarch (Gen. 25:8), says, "he was gathered to his kin." Like his predecessors, the man who dies becomes one of the fathers, a name in the genealogical list; and as such he never ceases to be a part of the continuing story of the People.[7]

This frame of mind made quite inconceivable the question of an individual afterlife and probably contributed to the fact that Hebrew thought never developed a notion of a soul or life-force which is separable from the historical man.[8] At the same time, the general Old Testament conceptualization is both different from and more profound than the Greek view of political immortality. The Greek notion seems to have been that immortality was earned through one's contribution to the state and that the locus of immortality was in the collective memory of the state. The Hebrew understanding is at once more primitive and more organic. Personality and identity are terms which attach not to the person but to the People; thus, when one dies, personality and identity are not disrupted, for the People continues. Only the possibility that one's line may not be fruitful gives rise to anxiety in the face of death.

In a general way, the kind of view expressed by the Yahwist historian persevered throughout the period of Old Testament writing. The concept of corporate personality tended to be refined (some might say, refined away), but the tradition refrained from assigning to death more than physiological significance and continued to regard the People as the locus both of continuity and of the ultimate meaning of life.

After the fall of the Israelite kingdoms and the period of the exiles, nevertheless, the historical situation of the Jews gave rise to a quite different formulation of the relationship between Yahweh and his People. No longer a member of a nation chosen from among the peoples of the world to fulfill a special calling, the Jew now found himself "essentially an *individual* adrift in the cosmos." [9] The older literature was canonized and reinterpreted so as to provide guidelines for the Jew in this dilemma, and new forms of religious writing emerged to give similar guidance and encouragement.

Chief among these kinds of writings are those of the Wisdom school. Most of the motifs of this literature are found elsewhere in the traditions of the ancient Near East, and they were not unknown to the Hebraic world before the fall of the kingdoms. But the Wisdom tradition came into its own as a theological and literary approach to the problems raised by the new historical situation of the Jews. Psalm 137 is the classic depiction of that situation: the People are captives in an alien land, longing for the familiar ways of Jerusalem (the ways whose importance had been explained by the Yahwist and other epics of the emergence of the People) and not knowing how to worship their God in the foreign place. The situation necessitated a new formulation of the religion (which we know as Judaism) which would guide the individual by instruction and by example and enable him to maintain his integrity in the face of his aloneness in the cosmos.

Thus, it is that the Wisdom literature is characterized both by a prescriptiveness which stresses the manner in which the wise man will react to his situation and by a resignation which counsels him to keep the faith in the face of adversity. In its approach to the phenomenon of death, the Wisdom school generally maintained the realism of the Yahwist historian. But the historical hopes of the Yahwist have been dashed: the People is no longer a nation whose emergence and reason for being need to be explained; the individual finds himself without a nation and seeks to understand the nature of his dependence upon Yahweh. Since he has no new picture of the meaning of death, the Wisdom writer tends to counsel resignation and trust in the face of death and other adversities, as in Job. Only occasionally did the school tend toward bitterness over the prospect of the end of life, as in Ecclesiastes and (more characteristically) Psalm 88.

The same phenomena which gave currency to the Wisdom literature gave rise to the apocalyptic literature in which pseudonymous wise men revealed the secrets of the future inbreaking of the divine realm upon the sphere of human life in order to save men. In the book Daniel, [10] for example, the central figure is portrayed as a wise man living among foreigners but strictly adherent to the Law of his People. The visions of Daniel reveal that the Son of Man will come from the heavenly to the human realm for the purpose of redeeming the latter and counsel the faithful to suffer martyrdom rather than gainsay the commandments and lose their place among the elect.

One of the characteristic teachings of apocalyptic (based ultimately upon extrapolations from certain of the Exilic and post-Exilic prophetic books) is the doctrine of resurrection. Whereas Ezekiel, in the vision of the valley of the dry bones (chapter 37), had spoken metaphorically of the restoration of the nation from its deathlike desolation, the writer of Daniel speaks of the resurrection of those Jews who have died in the interim between the collapse of the kingdoms and the forthcoming revival through Yahweh's agency. But this is not his only innovation. Influenced by the priestly notion that salvation depends upon one's adherence to the law (a notion which also tends to undermine the concept of corporate personality), the author also foresees a judgment of those who are raised: "And many of those who sleep in the dust of the earth shall awake, some to everlasting life, and some to shame and everlasting contempt. And those who are wise shall shine like the brightness of the firmament; and those who turn many to righteousness, like the stars for ever and ever" (Dan. 12:2-3 RSV).

Daniel does not, it must be noted, base this hope of a post-mortem life upon some notion of the nature of man but upon his faith that, in the divine economy, wisdom and virtue must be rewarded. And he can only conceive of this life as a corporate one within a restored and transformed Israel. His view is radically new, but it is also clearly continuous with the traditions of his heritage. It amounts to saying that one's life is not in vain if it is virtuous because, like the life of Abraham and others before, it has its meaning and continuation in the ongoing history of the People. To be dead or with one's kin is not to have become nothing, for the People will be restored. In this sense, Daniel simply reaffirms the tradition in which the Preacher had seen no grounds for continued confidence. Death gave no more grounds for anxiety to Daniel than to Abraham.[11]

THE NEW TESTAMENT

Much of New Testament teaching [12] concerning death developed from the apocalypticism of the Old Testament and the Apocrypha. Yet, it is a mistake to say that Jesus' teaching follows the spirit of apocalyptic eschatology, which tended to point to the exact time when the divine, restorative intervention might be expected.[13] Rather, Jesus maintained a careful tension between present and future: his proclamation of the imminent futurity of the Kingdom of God, combined with his assertions of the power and significance of his own work, is meant to state that "he who will bring in the Kingdom of God in the future has appeared in the present in Jesus himself, and in him the powers of the coming aeon are already at work. . . ." [14] Thus, more than that of the apocalyptic school, Jesus' eschatology is unconcerned with speculation concerning the meaning of death or the future destiny of the person.

There is, indeed, no passage in the Synoptic Gospels in which Jesus discourses explicitly on the subject of death. The questions which we characteristically ask about the subject simply did not occur to him or to those who gathered his sayings. It is possible, however, to deduce certain aspects of his attitude on the matter of death from several discourses whose chief subjects were quite different. In the following passage, for example, the intent of Jesus' interlocutors was to confound him by posing an impossible and hypothetical legal question:

"Teacher, Moses wrote for us that if a man's brother dies and leaves a wife, but leaves no child, the man must take the wife, and raise up children for his brother. There were seven brothers; the first took a wife, and when he died left no children; and the second took her, and died, leaving no children; and the third likewise; and the seven left no children. Last of all the woman also died. In the resurrection whose wife will she be? For the seven had her as wife."

Jesus said to them, "Is not this why you are wrong, that you know neither the scriptures nor the power of God? For when they rise from the dead, they neither marry nor are given in marriage, but are like angels in heaven. And as for the dead being raised, have you not read in the book of Moses, in the passage about the bush, how God said to him, 'I am the God of Abraham, and the God of Isaac, and the God of Jacob'? He is not God of the dead, but of the living; you are quite wrong." (Mark 12:18-27 RSV)[15]

Despite the fact that this passage is concerned with a question of legal interpretation, rather than an expostulation on the meaning of death, it will suit our present purpose of examining Jesus' attitude toward death. He does not speak on the subject directly or because death as a topic interests him. Rather it arises as an incident of an effort to entrap him in heretical teaching. He and the Sadducees are agreed on one point: that human life is to be conceived as a unitive phenomenon in which the physical and that which animates the physical (the Greeks would have called it spirit or soul) are inseparable. No more than the Abraham of the Yahwist historian can Jesus or his interlocutors imagine that body and soul are separable or that, as Socrates put it in the *Phaedo*, human life is a condition in which the soul is temporarily entrapped in flesh. Man is that being who exists on the historical plane and whose existence has both a beginning and an end.

But the Sadducees, who did not accept the apocalyptists' doctrine of resurrection, tried to confute that notion by resort to the device of *reductio ad absurdum* with their presentation of the impossible case of the woman married successively to seven brothers; and Jesus parried the question neatly. The doctrine of resurrection in Daniel had been an effort to say that life lived well was not in vain even though it bore no apparent fruit because of the present condition of the People. God would not allow such a life to be "vanity" as the Preacher of Ecclesiastes had thought, but would accept it into the genealogy of the restored Israel. It would be judged acceptable at the coming time of restoration or renewal. "He is not God of the dead, but of the living," and therefore, the literalistic question about life after the resurrection is absurdly beside the point. The God who manifested himself to Moses at the burning bush is concerned with the life of a People, the progeny of Abraham, and not with death.

What exactly Jesus conceived to be the nature of the life of resurrection is unclear, and it is unlikely that he ever considered the problem. His preoccupation was with the urgency of life in the present time: with the signs in his own ministry and in general historical phenomena which proclaimed or would soon proclaim that God is about to do something new, to inaugurate his kingship in a decisive way. This is the motif of the parables,[16] and the Synoptic Apocalypse[17] stresses not resurrection but the signs of the end of the present age. The statement: "And then he will send out the angels, and gather his elect from the four winds, from the ends of the earth to the ends of heaven" (Mark 13:27 RSV) is the only sentence (in only two of the three versions) of the Apocalypse which touches on resurrection; and it is very general. The description of the Last Judgment in Matthew 25:31-46 is cast in parabolic form so as to stress rather the importance of being prepared for the impending coming of God's kingship than the nature of the resurrection and its aftermath.[18]

Jesus, in other words, was unconcerned with speculations either about death or about the meaning of resurrection. Nothing he says seems to enlarge upon the traditional Hebraic stance; indeed, he seems to have used the language of apocalyptic while withdrawing from the apocalyptic picture of resurrection in favor of a reaffirmation of the kind of assertion made before the historical dislocation of the People. At the time of his crucifixion, there is abundant evidence in the Synoptic Gospels that Jesus showed both fear and terror in the face of suffering. Unlike Socrates, who faced death with triumphant composure, he took death as a terrible and serious thing.[19] His ultimate appeal was to the will of God, and that same will was his only and bitter comfort.

Jesus was concerned with life, or with the quality of life expected by God of his people, because he believed that the new age was about to begin. Death is the end of historical existence except insofar as one conceives of the dead as being with the fathers or a part of the living heritage of the People. To say that the dead shall be raised is to say that they will, as a part of the living heritage, participate in the life of the restored People which is about to begin.[20]

Of course, Jesus may have had (and probably did have) a more concrete picture than this in mind when he spoke of resurrection. His failure to be much more specific in his pronouncements is, however, made clear by the problems raised almost immediately for his followers in communicating this crucial, eschatological aspect of his teaching. For one thing, the time of the coming of the new order of things, for which Jesus had urged men to prepare, was not so imminent. Thus (rather as the Wisdom and apocalyptic schools emerged to answer questions raised by the historical failure of the expectations of the Hebraic peoples), it became imperative to develop a rationale for life in the interim before the coming of the kingship of God. Furthermore, it was necessary to accommodate Jesus' teaching, addressed only to the Jews, to the universal audience to whom Paul and others came to believe it was appropriate. And, finally, as a consequence of this, a new language was needed to express uniquely Judaic concepts in a society for which the terminology of the followers of Plato was more readily comprehensible.

It is in the writing of Paul, [21] who was attempting to resolve all three of these problems, that the problem of eschatology and the problem of death and the afterlife met and for the first time were made inseparable. Clarification of Jesus' vagueness, the lapse of time and the difficulty of cross-cultural interpretation all loom large in the following passage, which gathers a number of themes familiar in Paul's day and fuses them for the first time.

. . . There is one glory of the sun, and another glory of the moon, and another glory of the stars; for star differs from star in glory.

So it is with the resurrection of the dead. What is sown is perishable, what is raised is imperishable. It is sown in dishonor, it is raised in glory. It is sown in weakness, it is raised in power. It is sown a physical body, it is raised a spiritual body. If there is a physical body, there is also a spiritual body. Thus it is written, "The first man Adam became a living being"; the last Adam became a life-giving spirit. . . . I tell you this, brethren: flesh and blood cannot inherit the kingdom of God, nor does the perishable inherit the imperishable.

Lo! I tell you a mystery. We shall not all sleep, but we shall all be changed, in a moment, in the twinkling of an eye, at the last trumpet. For the trumpet will sound, and the dead will be raised imperishable, and we shall be changed. For this perishable nature must put on the imperishable, and this mortal nature must put on immortality. When the perishable puts on the imperishable, and the mortal puts on immortality, then shall come to pass the saying that is written:

> "Death is swallowed up in victory."
> "O death, where is thy victory?
> O death, where is thy sting?" (I Cor. 15: 41-55 RSV)

No longer can the question of the nature of the resurrection as a mode of existence for the revivified dead be evaded. It must become what it was only potentially in the apocalyptic tradition: a special kind of corporeal existence which is a reward for the righteous who have died and a punishment for the wicked. To spell out what he means by this, Paul has recourse not only to fundamentally Greek terms like "spiritual" but also to the typological comparison of Christ and Adam and to the logical forms of disputation familiar to the philosophical schools and through them, perhaps, to the rabbinical schools of the Jewish dispersion. The passage is primarily a careful, rhetorical, and logical development of the antitheses of "physical" and "spiritual," constructed so as to show that there can be full life (in the unitive, Hebraic sense) for those who will be raised but that it must be understood symbolically or spiritually (in the dualistic Greek sense) as radically different from historical existence. Just as Jesus was raised, so all men will be raised—or, if they are still living, changed—when the time comes. Therefore, the length of the time interval makes little difference; salvation remains universally available.[22]

Death in Paul's view is the "last" and greatest enemy of man, yet an enemy whose power derives from man's own acts of sinfulness. The moment of death is, thus, one of obliteration or of self-obliteration but for the intervention of God in Christ Jesus, whose own resurrection and glorification constitutes man's only hope of victory over death (I Cor. 15:12-

22). Death is, then, an event or phenomenon of awful seriousness; Jesus' own reactions to his impending death were not cowardly or unphilosophical but absolutely realistic. But Jesus' own triumph is the assurance of man's triumph whenever God chooses to inaugurate his own reign. Those who die in Christ are, euphemistically, "asleep" and awaiting the ultimate triumph—or the dread judgment—at the resurrection with the rest of the People of God. Ultimately, the dead will be raised, corporeal and yet spiritual; and therefore, we can face death with a sure hope of ultimate triumph by God's grace.

With the possible exception of the radically Hellenized Wisdom of Solomon of the Apocrypha, the first consistently developed theology of death in the Judeo-Christian intellectual tradition is that of Paul. Although none of Paul's assumptions were novel in the first century, he seems to have gone beyond what Jesus said on the subject, so far as we can tell from the meager record of the Gospels; and he makes certain concessions in its vocabulary, at least, to common Greek conceptualizations. But the expansions and the concessions are minimal and were necessary in the light of the apologetic problems of explaining the lengthening of the interim and of speaking to a non-Judaic audience. The fundamental elements of the tradition—the lack of distinction between body and spirit and the overriding concern not with the destiny of the individual but with that of the People—are carefully maintained to the absolute exclusion of either the dualistic and metaphysical or the political notion of immortality which the Hellenistic Age had inherited from fifth-century Greece.

Statements like that of Geoffrey Gorer, that "orthodox Christianity is dogmatic that the soul continues to exist after death," [23] are, then, absolutely without biblical foundation. Not only do the biblical writers on the whole have no conception of a soul as a separable element of human existence, but also there is agreement that death is the (often dreadful) termination of existence and that there is no such thing as an individual afterlife. The very urgency of living well in the world arises, in the biblical outlook, from the fact of death and from the high mission of the People of the Covenant, old or new, within which People alone the individual's life has meaning and purpose. At the end of the biblical tradition, the Pauline emphasis upon the general resurrection serves simply to underline these points, that all life is corporeal and that the judgment of mankind is general because the People is indivisible. In this view lay the possibility of a further development in which man could be regarded as entering upon an afterlife in the body of his resurrection after the sleep of the interim.

Against this general understanding of death, the Greek views stand in contrast. Whereas the Judeo-Christians maintained the unity of the human being, the Greek philosophical tradition in general conceived of a soul which might or must continue to exist after its separation from the body. Metaphysically speaking, immortality was a necessary logical deduction for the Greek but an inconceivable construct for the Jews and primitive Christians. And, whereas the Hebraic progenitor was understood as always part of the living heritage of the People, the Greek political hero continued to exist in the memory of his city and thus to be granted immortality.

The history of early Christian reflection on the meaning of death is an important part of the story of the confrontation of the Hebraic tradition with the Hellenistic, to which this review of developing views of death and the afterlife must now turn.

3 THE GREEK PATRISTIC TRADITION

FOR THE TIME BEING, it will be necessary to set aside the stream of the pre-Christian Greek tradition, which viewed immortality as a gift of the city to its heroes. It had little influence on early Christianity, except as it may have influenced the cult of saints, who were the heroes of the Christian *polis,* and as it provided the impetus for the cult of the Emperor and thereby occasioned the major conflict between the Christians and the Empire. So far as this survey has gone, it serves primarily as a contrast to the Hebraic understanding of death.

It is the stream of Greek thought which conceived metaphysically of immortality and had its chief source in Plato which must now occupy our attention, for channeled through the successor schools of philosophy at Athens and Alexandria, it came to exercise a direct and crucial influence upon Christian thought concerning death and the afterlife.[1]

IRENAEUS OF LYONS

At first, this influence was felt indirectly. The Hellenistic world had thoroughly assimilated the notion of a cosmic dualism which inevitably gave rise to the idea of a soul which is the immortal part of man and continues to exist in a disembodied state after it has been freed from the body. These ideas had come to be accepted almost without challenge in every quarter of the Mediterranean basin, and their appearance in popular religious thought need not be directly or immediately related to recent philosophical developments. Even Judaism seems to have been affected. In the wake of the final dashing of the political hopes of the Jews with the destruction of Jerusalem by the Romans, A.D. 70, the apocalyptic dream had been shattered; and these events gave reinforcement to the impulse which had begun to view salvation in terms of a radically dualistic escape from history rather than as an event within or at the culmination of history. Thus, it was in Gnosticism that the eschatological teaching of the early church met its first challenge.[2] Gnosticism was essentially unphilosophical in its excessive dualism and is in many respects a travesty upon the intellectual tradition of the Greeks;[3] but in the conflict of the Christians with the Gnostics, the basic arguments which would also serve to maintain the Hebraic view of man and the meaning of death were forged.

The most important spokesman against the Gnostics was Irenaeus, who became Bishop of Lyons, in Gaul, about A.D. 177.[4] In the *Refutation and Overthrow of Knowledge, Falsely So Called* (usually, and more conveniently, cited as *Against Heresies*), Irenaeus undertook a lengthy exposé and refutation of the several Gnostic schools and a restatement of the doctrine of salvation.

In the midst of the fifth book, he comes to the problem of the fate of man between his death and the general resurrection:

If, then, the Lord observed the law of the dead, that He might become the first-begotten from the dead, and tarried until the third day "in the lower parts of the earth," then afterwards rising in the flesh, so that He even showed the print of the nails to His disciples, He thus ascended to the Fathers [if all these things occurred, I say], how must these men not be put to confusion, who allege that "the lower parts" refers to this world of ours, but that their inner man, leaving the body here, ascends into the supercelestial place? For as the Lord "went away in the midst of the shadow of death," where the souls of the dead were, yet afterwards arose in the body, and after the resurrection was taken up [into heaven], it is manifest that the souls of His disciples also, upon whose account the Lord underwent these things, shall go away into the invisible place allotted to them by God, and there remain until the resurrection, awaiting that event; then receiving their bodies, and rising in their entirety, that is bodily, just as the Lord arose, they shall come thus into the presence of God. "For no disciple is above the Master, but every one that is perfect shall be as his Master." As our Master, therefore, did not at once depart, taking flight [to heaven], but awaited the time of His resurrection prescribed by the Father, which had been also shown forth through Jonas, and rising again after three days was taken up [to heaven]; so ought we also to await the time of our resurrection prescribed by God and foretold by the prophets, and so, rising, be taken up, as many as the Lord shall account worthy of this [privilege].[5]

The first thing to be noticed about this passage from Irenaeus is that, unlike the biblical writings, it seems to imply a doctrine of the soul. If it is only an implication of the passages concerning the descent of Christ to "where the souls of the dead were" and of the notion that Christ's disciples must wait in a like manner, it is made explicit elsewhere in *Against Heresies*. But Irenaeus' understanding of the nature of the soul, carefully worked out in contradistinction to that of the Gnostics, is severely limited. Attacking the Platonic teachings of the transmigration of souls and recollection,[6] he argues that the soul continues to exist after it has been separated from the body but that, created in order to animate that same body, its only recollection is of its physical or created existence and its only form that in which it was united with the body.[7] In yet another passage, Irenaeus considers in greater detail the composition of man. He is body, soul, and spirit—the latter element being the divine life-principle. These elements are indispensable if he is to be saved: "Now the soul and the spirit are certainly a *part* of the man, but certainly not *the* man; for the perfect man consists in the commingling and the union of the soul receiving the spirit of the Father, and the admixture of that fleshly nature which was moulded after the image of God." [8] It is clear that Irenaeus puts more stress in passages of this sort on spirit than on soul, for he believed that this element allowed for the perfectability of man and the release of the soul from carnality.[9] It is the body which is mortal; but the soul or "breath of life" is incorporeal and immortal, and the spirit is simple and not susceptible to decomposition.[10]

These beliefs take Irenaeus well beyond Paul in terms of the extent to which he accepts as inescapable the Hellenistic duality of soul and body. He and most of his contemporaries began their theological careers with this dualism as a presupposition. The unitive Hebraic understanding of man was, almost from the first, discarded; and it did not occur to this leader of the attack on heretical dualism to reaffirm the ancient Israelite view, which by the second century was already inconceivable. But the views of Irenaeus and other early churchmen were strikingly original from the Greek point of view as well. Salvation for Irenaeus was not a matter of release of the soul from the body to an incorporeal state from which it may originally have come but of reunion of body and soul at the resurrection.

The passage quoted at the head of this section is central both to Irenaeus' doctrine of salvation and to his understanding of death. Death is for him the beginning of an indeterminate or suspended state for the soul which must last until the body is raised. In his soteriology, the experience of Christ is said to recapitulate all of history and the experience of each individual. Thus, the descent into hell is to Christ what the period between death and resurrection is to all other men. Jesus died, physically and as all men die—a concept absolutely repugnant to the Gnostics. His body in the grave, his soul was "where the souls of the dead were." When he rose, it was in the body which showed the marks of his violent death, and in the same condition he ascended into heaven. The same must be the fate of Jesus' followers, although the interim will be longer than three days. There is no tendency in Irenaeus' treatment of the matter to ascribe any kind of activity to the souls which await the resurrection. At one place,[11] he does remark that the souls of the dead dwell in conditions accordant to the qualities of their lives, but the comment is isolated and undeveloped.

Karl Rahner has said that the Platonic definition of death as the "separation of the body and the soul" was immediately taken over by the earliest Christians and is "used in such a matter-of-fact way . . . that we must consider and accept it as the classical theological description of death." [12] An analysis of Irenaeus' *Against Heresies* demonstrates both the truth of that statement and the severe limitations which must be put on its application. Irenaeus has gone beyond the biblical point of view, but he has also so severely limited the Hellenistic point of view as to leave it virtually unrecognizable in his effort to maintain the necessity of the salvation of the whole man. Body and soul are separated at death. But death is not the end of existence for the one and the beginning of real life for the other. Rather body and soul await their reunion and the beginning of perfected life in the coming kingdom. Salvation will not be complete until the Kingdom of God, which is both corporate and corporeal, has come into being.

ORIGEN

The work of Origen [13] in the first half of the third century comprises the first body of Christian theological writing by a man thoroughly conversant with Hellenistic philosophy. Origen was apparently recognized as a formidable figure in philosophical circles in Alexandria. The fact that he was a Christian and, therefore, employed unusual mythological references to the Judeo-Christian Scriptures seems to have been regarded only as an idiosyncrasy by some of the contemporary pagan philosophers. Trained by the same teacher under whom Plotinus worked, he attempted in his profoundly biblical theology to see his own religion as an allegory of Platonist philosophy. That this effort should have been made was inevitable in the third-century milieu; and, once taken, it was immeasurably influential among Origen's detractors as well as his admirers. The combination of philosophical Gnosticism, biblical mythology, and a profound piety achieved by the great Alexandrian teacher was the most creative and comprehensive theology of the patristic age.

The implications of Origen's work with regard to death are extremely important and cannot adequately be treated here both because they were, on the whole, rejected by later theologians and because they were so complicated that an adequate exposition would upset the balance of this volume.[14] Some effort to outline the teaching of Origen must, however, be attempted if only because it throws in bolder relief the efforts of a later generation of Greek theologians to recapture the biblical view while taking account of the Platonic world-picture.

Origen's mature reflections are recorded in the treatise *Against Celsus,* in which he answered the allegations of a pagan philosopher against Christianity. The following passage concerning the problem of resurrection should serve to illustrate the kinds of arguments mustered by non-Christians and the remarkable sophistication of Origen's own position:

> Therefore, we do not say that after the body has been corrupted it will *return to its original nature,* just as the grain of

corn that has been corrupted will not return to be a grain of corn. For we hold that, as from the grain of corn an ear rises up, so in the body there lies a certain principle which is not corrupted from which the body is raised in incorruption. . . . And we do not *escape to a most outrageous refuge by saying that anything is possible to God.* We know that we may not understand the word "anything" of things which do not exist or which are inconceivable. But we do say that *God cannot do what is shameful,* since then God could not possibly be God. For if God does anything shameful He is not God.

But when [Celsus] affirms that God also *does not desire that which is contrary to nature,* we have to make a distinction in his remark. If anyone says evil is what is contrary to nature, we also hold that God does not desire what is contrary to nature, neither that which is the result of sin, nor what is done irrationally. . . . If we are forced to use this terminology, we will say that compared with what is commonly regarded as nature some things which sometimes God might do transcend nature, such as lifting man up beyond human nature and making him change to a superior and more divine nature, and keeping him in this position for so long as the man who is kept shows by his actions that he desires Him to do this.[15]

One of the primary problems which Origen seeks to avoid in his theology is the dualism of good-evil, spiritual-physical, which pervades the teaching of the philosophers and of the Christian heretics. He does so by conceiving of the cosmos, much as did Plato, as having originally been created as a spiritual or nonphysical order which was at once rational and harmonious. But the rational spirits so generated were free and capable of change. They could remain in harmony with God or move away from that harmony. Some did move away, creating disorder by their fall. The physical creation represents the diversity and lack of order so brought into being. The work of Christ is to show man the way to return to his original harmony and spirituality in communion with God, who is Truth.

The education of the soul is for Origen, as for Plato, the goal of existence.[16] The soul must be purified or purged, as though by fire, of its tendency to misuse its freedom and must be led back to its proper state of pure spirituality.[17]

Within this view of the cosmos and of the nature of salvation, it would be foolish to conceive of death other than as a separation of the soul from physical matter or to think that the soul after this severance will be inactive or asleep. It must continue its journey of purification, hopefully moving by stages toward the source of all being, God.

It is also ridiculous to conceive of resurrection as a revivification of the cast-off flesh, for physical matter can have no role in the scheme of salvation. In the section quoted, Origen counters Celsus' accusation that Christians believe literally in a physical resurrection with a brilliant exegesis of I Corinthians 15 in which he stresses Paul's seed image. The thing produced from the planted seed is an essentially new thing. So, too, the body to be raised is not that which was buried and has rotted away but a new thing. The essential and indestructible aspect of man is the soul, or rational principle. Resurrection of the imperishable body becomes a metaphor for the clothing of that principle when the soul has attained salvation.

To insist otherwise is to assert that God would do what is contrary both to reason and to his nature. Origen's God is limited in this respect—or, rather, it is inconceivable to Origen that God should ever act against reason. What resurrection means, then, is that God raises man above man's nature and toward his own divinity by means of the education of the soul and that he restores man to that estate from which he has fallen. There, since souls will remain free, it is conceivable that the souls of men might fall again and bring into being new worlds and new occasions for saving acts.

It would be tempting to say that Origen's system is an intellectual *tour de force* if that were possible without demeaning his originality and his intellectual perspicacity and integrity.

He achieved a consistent presentation of what he took to be the essence of his faith in terms of the most advanced philosophical thought of his age. It is a work of genius, yet it was not a satisfactory solution to the basic problems of Christian theology.

Perhaps the core of the problem is Origen's conception of the essence of his faith. In the biblical traditions, salvation was regarded as a gift of God to his people. It is always described in terms of corporate restoration or reconstitution. In the thought of Origen, salvation is the restoration of souls to the state from which they have fallen. Thus, whatever one may say about the glory or the unity of souls, which will be effected once the restoration is achieved, attention is turned from the *goal* of salvation to the *process* of salvation and from the body of the saved, the People of God, to those individual souls that are seeking salvation.

Origen's work represents a remarkable effort to marry Christianity and the Platonic world-picture. It is a radical step beyond the accommodations to Hellenism made by his forerunners who, like Irenaeus, attempted carefully to maintain the Hebraic world-view at the same time as they accepted and adapted ideas like that of the soul. For all the profundity of his achievement as a biblical exegete and despite the moving biographical evidence of his sincere devotion to Christianity, Origen quite undermined the spirit of the faith to which he witnessed. Like Plato, he understood much of what he said as metaphor, as an attempt to picture the unimaginable or inexpressible.[18] But the poet-philosopher's vision is of a different New Jerusalem from that of the Scripture.

With regard to the problem of death and man's destiny, his recognition that Greek dualism was at odds with the monistic biblical assertion that God is the sole creator led him to a formulation in which the created order cannot be taken seriously. Thus, life and death are only the limits of one fairly insignificant state of an eternal journey of the soul as it moves away from or back toward the Truth, from which it derived its being.

GREGORY OF NYSSA

In the century after Origen, the questions which he had raised were answered in a form which was to become classical for the later Greek theological tradition by the so-called Cappadocian Fathers, Basil the Great, Gregory Nazianzus, and Gregory of Nyssa. It was the last, and the youngest, of these who addressed himself to the problem of death.

The dialogue *On the Soul and the Resurrection* is Gregory of Nyssa's most extended treatment of man's ultimate destiny. Written about A.D. 380, it is cast in the form of a last conversation between the Bishop of Nyssa and his sister, Macrina. Gregory had gone to visit Macrina because he was deeply troubled by the death of their brother Basil, but he found his sister herself near death. In the presence of her friends, Macrina and Gregory discuss at great length the matters of death and human destiny, the sister assuming the role of "teacher."

There is reason to believe that *On the Soul and the Resurrection* was written as a footnote to another treatise (itself intended to complete a study left unfinished by Basil) and actually represents a change in Gregory's viewpoint "in a more spiritual direction." [19] Yet the contrast between this document and the writing of Origen is startling. Whereas Origen had attempted to Platonize the biblical writings, Gregory takes pains to safeguard the biblical teachings from the encroachments of Greek notions of afterlife at the same time as he attempts to speak responsibly and intelligently to the intellectual community. The curious qualities of his results ought immediately to be apparent:

There is nothing . . . to hinder the soul's presence in the body's atoms, whether fused in union or decomposed in dissolution. Just as in the amalgam of gold and silver a certain methodical force is to be observed which has fused the metals, and if the one be afterwards smelted of the other, the law of this method nevertheless continues to reside in each, so that while the amalgam is separated this method does not suffer division with it (for you cannot make fractions out of the indivisible), in the same way this intelligent essence of the soul is observable in the concourse of the atoms, and does not undergo division when they are dissolved; but it remains with them, and even in their separation it is co-extensive with them, yet not itself dissevered nor discounted into sections to accord with the number of the atoms. Such a condition belongs to the material and spacial world, but that which is intelligent and undimensional is not liable to the circumstances of space. Therefore the soul exists in the actual atoms which she has once animated, and there is no force to tear her away from her cohesion with them. What cause for melancholy, then, is there herein, that the visible is exchanged for the invisible; and wherefore is it that your mind has conceived such a hatred of death? [20]

Gregory had opened his discussion with Macrina by posing questions concerning the existence and destiny of the soul. The soul, she replied, "is an essence created, and living, and intellectual, transmitting from itself to an organized and sentient body the power of living and of grasping objects of sense, as long as a natural constitution capable of this holds together." [21] It has "a rare and peculiar nature of its own" and is independent "of the body with its gross texture." [22] Inasmuch as man is a microcosm, "a little world in himself [containing] all the elements which go to create the universe," [23] the soul is the divine element in man and must be considered immortal.

In this context the passage quoted appears as a discussion of the meaning of death for the soul-body relationship. Since the soul is the vivifying force, Gregory believes that even after death "that bond of vivifying influence" will not vanish.[24] The soul and its body belong together and can never be free of each other. The soul must, therefore, always be with the body even though it no longer vivifies it; and yet the soul retains its immortality and integrity, for it does not depend on locality for its identity and being.

This basic premise is refined as the dialogue continues. In an excursus on the relation of the soul to the emotions, or passions, it is concluded that emotion is related to sensation and therefore to "brute creation" and that the value of emotion depends on the use to which it is put by human will.[25] When Gregory asks about Hades, he is told by Macrina that Hades is a "word for a place in which souls are said to be [and] means nothing else but a transition to that Unseen world of which we have no glimpse." [26] Since the soul is immaterial, there is no way to localize its existence after death, and speculation about the locus of its existence is futile.

Gregory then draws Macrina back to the mainstream of their discussion, asking how the soul will "follow" along with the destroyed body. The soul, Macrina replies, has the unique "power of recognition," which, for example, an artist has for that which he has created; and therefore it cannot fail to recognize its body either when it is decayed or at the resurrection.[27] To those who would object by citing the parable of Dives and Lazarus, she adds, it must be argued that the physical details of that story have to be translated to "an equivalent in the world of ideas." The Gospel parable says, simply, that the living must keep free of obsessive "attachments" to the fleshly lest, even in the disembodied state, they be subject to the same distractions.[28] Thus, there is a sense in which it may be said that the soul during the interim after death is still being drawn from evil to good. The good soul tends always toward the godhead, as though it were light drawn upward; but that which has been overly distracted by the life of the flesh tends toward the fleshly, as though it were heavy and pulled down.[29] In the light of the exegesis of the Lazarus parable, the physical imagery of this passage must be understood both metaphorically and as an accommodation to the doctrine of the progress of the soul. But it should be evident that Gregory is extremely cautious and is attempting to play down the notion of the soul's independent afterlife.

Finally, Gregory turns to the problem of resurrection, establishing the logical possibility of rejoining the soul and the body, treating the problem of evil and establishing the notion that the resurrection will occur when the perfect number of human souls has been attained.[30] Answering her brother's last objections, Macrina discusses the manner in which man is purged so that he can appear at Judgment in a state of incorruption.[31]

It should be clear from this summary of *On the Soul and the Resurrection* that Gregory of Nyssa, standing in the Platonic tradition of philosophy and at the end of the Greek patristic tradition, has steadfastly refused to speculate about the status of the soul between death and resurrection. Body and soul are in a strange but real way inseparable. The immortality of the soul is a premise, but it is radically interpreted in the light of the resurrection. Immortality is a source of consolation for the living as they contemplate death, but hope is primarily aimed at the time beyond temporality when the perfect number of souls will have been created, and, purged of all evil, incorrupt man will dwell eternally in body and soul with God.

It has frequently been remarked that the situation depicted in Gregory's dialogue closely resembles that of the *Phaedo* of Plato.[32] Nyssa chose to model his work on the most famous and most important classical treatment of the immortality of the soul and the afterlife. Thus, he sets the Christian doctrine in bold contrast with the philosophical. Most explicitly, he rejects Plato's notions of reincarnation, immediate judgment after death, and the ultimate separability of soul and body. These notions were, of course, treated as mythology by Plato; [33] but, even so, they were fundamentally incompatible with the Christian position and had to be answered. Indeed, it may be that the implied contradiction of the Platonic tradition in *On the Soul and the Resurrection* is as significant as the more immediate criticism of Origen's tendency to overemphasize the importance of the separability of the soul from the body.[34] At any rate, the pattern of Gregory's eschatology is clearly biblical rather than Platonic.

It is difficult and even dangerous to attempt to summarize the conclusions of the Greek Fathers with regard to the problem of death both because of the diversity of their views and because of the complexity of their philosophical presuppositions. On the whole, however, it can be said that they accepted the idea of the immortality of the soul as a useful tool for treating that which is unique in man's being and nature. Faced, however, with the clear—and to the Greek intellectual, outrageous—biblical conception of man as being asleep or at rest from his death to the general resurrection, the notion of the immortal soul was as much an encumbrance as a help. It was difficult to avoid the implication that the soul had some independent existence or goal once it was freed of the body. Nevertheless, both the early apologist Irenaeus and the theologian-bishop Gregory of Nyssa seem conscious of this difficulty and are at pains to avoid it. In Origen, we see what might have been. The very fact that Christian teachers in general rejected Origen's massive, masterful, and cohesive system is testimony to the staying force of the biblical view. Had Origen prevailed, Christians would immediately have endorsed a view of death as a relatively minor event in a continuing process of purification for the soul. As it was, death continued to be regarded as the beginning of a period of inactivity for both body and soul, which simply await the great common hour of salvation, when all are raised or changed.

4 THE LATIN PATRISTIC TRADITION

THE INFLUENCE OF THE EARLY CHRISTIAN THEOLOGIANS who wrote in Greek upon those who wrote in Latin was great. Throughout the patristic period, the Latin Christian writers followed the lead of the Greeks at every turn. Nevertheless—almost as though one could attribute different mentalities to the two chief linguistic divisions of the Roman Empire—the Latin writers subtly transformed whatever they received, giving it quite different emphases.

One note of the biblical tradition which is virtually ignored by the Greek Fathers is that of judgment. In the Hebraic tradition, at least from the time of the Deuteronomic reform of the late seventh century B.C., the historic destiny of the People always depended upon the judgment of Yahweh on its history. Wisdom often stresses the seeming abandonment of the People by its God and yearns for some gracious act as a sign of forgiveness. Apocalyptic emphasizes its faith that God will vindicate his People by an act of restoration and a judgment of the oppressing nations. Both regard the present tribulations as divine judgment upon the faithless Chosen People. A key element of the universalism of the New Testament and of primitive Christianity was the belief that the resurrection was inseparable from a universal judgment of mankind based upon the quality of men's response to the Gospel. Thus, originally, a post-mortem judgment of man's life in the world was an integral element of the expected resurrection and the inauguration of the Kingdom of God.

The pervasive influence of the Platonic notion of the soul

upon the Greek Fathers tended to eclipse this element of the Gospel. Whatever reservations they expressed concerning the Platonists' picture of the post-mortem destiny of the soul, the early Greek theologians nevertheless tended to view the whole history of human existence in terms of the effort to educate the soul so as to lead it back toward Truth and an ultimate, restored existence in the presence of Truth. Judgment tended to be an examination of the soul to determine how far it had advanced in its education. Thus, and not only in the system of Origen, the salvation offered by the Christ was regarded as a universal, cosmic salvation, a restoration of all souls to their proper condition, from which they had fallen. At the end of the educative process, there would be none left to be consigned to "outer darkness." Resurrection was carefully guarded as the uniquely Christian doctrine of salvation, but very often it was interpreted not as a picture of the end of man but as a metaphor for the salvation of souls.

Christian and non-Christian, the Latin-speaking peoples were greatly influenced by the Greek doctrine of the soul, which became a part of the basic intellectual equipment at both ends of the Empire. But the Latin mind, like the Hebraic, was deeply concerned with the processes of history and with the moral implications of action within history. The destiny of the soul, thus, came to be envisioned in terms of justice or of the consequences of the quality of the human life, which preceded the separation of soul and body.

The contrast is perhaps best shown by comparing the conclusions of two of the most important documents of antiquity, both of which deal with the destiny of the soul and relate that fate to political life in the body. Plato's *Republic,* the first of these, ends with the vision of Er of the underworld, in which he learns, much as in the *Phaedo,* that souls will meet various fates according to their state of enlightenment.[1] The lesson that Plato has Socrates say at the end is that man must always pursue truth and enlightenment, keeping his soul unsullied. Thus, man's ordering of his earthly life—and especially of its political aspects—will affect the destiny of the soul. The good *polis* is that which is so ordered as to promote the education of its citizens, to contribute to the progressive enlightenment of their souls. Hence, the famous Platonic dictum that philosophers are the best kings. Life, then, is useful only in so far as it is devoted to the education of the soul.

The Roman counterpart of Plato's vision occurs at the end of the *Republic* of Marcus Tullius Cicero, which was written consciously as a sequel to the work of the Athenian philosopher. Scipio, who plays in Cicero's dialogue a role comparable to that of Socrates, tells of a dream [2] in which he had a glimpse of the next world. Although the content of Scipio's dream is approximately the same as that of Er, its treatment is subtly different so that virtue becomes an end in itself and is rewarded by a joyful eternal existence for the soul. No longer is the education of the soul and its reunion with truth the primary focus. Rather virtuous, active life in the earthly city is the ultimate value, and it is rewarded by the gift of perpetual bliss for the soul. The good state is that which promotes virtue so that the souls of both its leaders and its citizens can reap the rewards.

Thus, human life could acquire a tone of urgency in Roman thought which differed importantly from the attitude of the Greeks toward life in history. History and human action in history, morally judged, are inextricably connected with the destiny of the immortal soul. The body may be the prison of the soul in Roman as in Greek metaphors, but it is the historical, embodied person who, by valor and virtuousness, wins salvation for his soul.

TERTULLIAN

The effects of this special Roman view upon theological thought are evident immediately in the work of the first Latin

Christian writer, Tertullian of Carthage. The African lawyer and rhetorician, who lived in the late-second and early-third centuries, exhibits in his treatise *On the Resurrection of the Flesh* both a tendency to stress the judgmental aspect of the resurrection and a willingness to consider the possibility of a punishment of the soul between death and resurrection:

> The entire cause, then, or rather necessity of the resurrection, will be this, namely, that arrangement of the final judgment which shall be most suitable to God. Now, in effecting this arrangement, you must consider whether the divine censure superintends a judicial examination of the two natures of man—both his soul and his flesh. For that which is a suitable object to be judged, is also a competent one to be raised. . . . Now, since the entire man consists of the union of the two natures, he must therefore appear in both, as it is right that he should be judged in his entirety; nor, of course, did he pass through life except in his entire state. As therefore he lived, so also must he be judged, because he has to be judged concerning the way in which he lived. For life is the cause of judgment, and it must undergo investigation in as many natures as it possessed when it discharged its vital functions. . . .
>
> . . . That souls are even now susceptible of torment and of blessing in Hades, though they are disembodied, and notwithstanding their banishment from the flesh, is proved by the case of Lazarus. . . . Therefore as it has acted in each several instance, so proportionably does [the soul] suffer in Hades, being the first to taste of judgment as it was the first to induce to the commission of sin; but still it is waiting for the flesh in order that it may through the flesh also compensate for its deeds. . . . This, in short, will be the process of that judgment which is postponed to the last great day, in order that by the exhibition of the flesh the entire course of the divine vengeance may be accomplished.[3]

If *On the Resurrection of the Flesh* were his only work touching on the subject of death, one might be justified in feeling that, had the resurrection of the body not already been a Christian doctrine, Tertullian might have taught it as a necessary corollary to his sense of the divine justice. Shortly before the passage quoted, Tertullian speaks of the treatise so far as it has progressed as "my eulogy of the flesh, in opposition to its enemies." [4] The piece is, in other words, a polemic against the Gnostics and others who hold the body in low repute. No less is it aimed against the Docetists, who regarded the body of Christ as an illusion. Never one to understate his position, Tertullian tends in his "eulogy" to take a radical position on the value of the physical man which conflicts at some points with the similarly extreme stand which he assumed in the companion piece, *On the Soul.* And always it is the polemical or apologetic occasion for writing which shapes the outcome more than abstract or systematic goals. Here even the title is extreme in its use of the term "flesh" for the more usual "body."

The rigorism of African Christianity in general and of Tertullian in particular—developed against the background of persecution—always tended toward apocalypticism.[5] In the case of the first great Latin theologian, the rigoristic inclination was so strong that he ultimately allied himself with the Montanist schism. A sense of the necessity of judgment is always inherent among religious and moralistic rigorists. Tertullian's strong belief in historical and ultimate punishment and reward are such that even the sternest of the Old Testament prophets do not overreach him. Man must be responsible for what he has wrought; and the vicissitudes of this present life, although they are certainly not distinct from the system of retributive justice, are not sufficient to embrace the entire significance of divine judgment.

Thus, first, there is the soul to be considered. For Tertullian even more than Irenaeus its existence is axiomatic and scriptural. Following the Stoics, Tertullian insists that it is a material substance—as, indeed, in some sense is God as well—: ". . . the soul is corporeal, possessing a peculiar kind of solidity in its nature, such as enables it both to perceive and suffer." [6] At the same time as he adopts the general Hellenistic picture of the soul, Tertullian incongruously blends with it another metaphysical picture which makes it possible for the soul to suffer the consequences or to enjoy the rewards of its mode of historical behavior.[7] And thus, too, this first Latin theological corpus puts unusual emphasis upon the fate of the soul immediately after its separation from the body.[8] It is the lawyer's distinct feeling that divine justice demands that to conceive of the soul as going free until the resurrection would be to allow it to get away with what it does not deserve. Therefore, it must be punished or rewarded.[9] The "exile in Hades" [10] is conceived as an active state, and it was improvised to do service to Tertullian's strict sense of justice.

Nevertheless, it is clear that the major thrust of the theology of Tertullian regarding man's fate after death is not to emphasize the destiny of the soul at the expense of the traditional teaching concerning the resurrection of the body. Just as it would be unjust to think of the soul as waiting idly for the Last Day, it is unjust to believe that God does not take seriously the flesh of man and intend to reward or punish it. Man is body and spirit, and he must stand trial "in his entire state." The resurrection is not so much the mode of the restoration of Israel or of the inauguration of a new, perfected order of being but rather the occasion of the execution of divine justice. The quality of the everlasting life after the Judgment receives only cursory treatment and is of secondary interest.[11]

The apocalyptic picture painted by Tertullian underlines the urgency of living well in present history. The way in which man responds to the hardships of history, to the trials of persecution, and to the demand of absolute righteousness will determine his destiny. The issue is "whether he has taken care or not to acknowledge and honour his Lord and Creator. . . ." [12] Death is inevitably the beginning of a judgment of life, of the quality of the living response to the way of the Gospel. So the soul must suffer or enjoy its reward. But historical life is physical and spiritual: ". . . the flesh is the very condition on which salvation hinges. And since the soul is, in consequence of its salvation, chosen to the service of God, it is the flesh which actually renders it capable of such service."[13] Salvation is just recompense for embodied life in the world, and it cannot be complete until body and soul, man in his entirety, stand before the bar of justice.

Tertullian's uniquely Latin point of view, then, radically affects his view of death and its consequences. Life in history assumes a new and unique importance which encourages rather more stress upon the proximate destiny of the soul. But, at the same time, the resurrection takes on far greater importance than for any of the Greek Fathers as the only occasion for full judgment. If Tertullian undermines the careful distance maintained elsewhere in the theological tradition between the day of death and the day of Judgment and opens the door to greater emphasis upon the activities of the disembodied soul, he also endows the resurrection with a crucial function in the economy of justice which restores to historical life the sense of urgency which is lacking in the more abstract and rationalistic approaches of the Greek Fathers.

AUGUSTINE OF HIPPO

Like Origen, Augustine plays so crucial a role in the history of Christian thought that no survey can do justice to his achievement.[14] There is, however, one convenient, late book of Augustine's, the *Enchiridion* of about A.D. 421, in which his mature views are conveniently and reflectively summarized. The work is an exposition of the Lord's Prayer and the Creed, and its final chapters contain the materials pertinent to this inquiry into reflections about death.

Now, for the time that intervenes between man's death and the final resurrection, there is a secret shelter for his soul, as each is worthy of rest or affliction according to what it has merited while it lived in the body. . . .

After the resurrection, however, when the general judgment has been held and finished, the boundary lines will be set for the two cities: the one of Christ, the other of the devil; one for the good, the other for the bad—both including angels and men. In the one group, there will be no will to sin, in the other, no power to sin, nor any further possibility of dying. The citizens of the first commonwealth will go on living truly and happily in life eternal. The second will go on, miserable in death eternal, with no power to die to it. The condition of both societies then will be fixed and endless. But in the first city, some will outrank others in bliss, and in the second, some will have a more tolerable burden of misery than others.[15]

As for Tertullian, the problem of the judgment of man's performance in history, or man's response to the gracious offer of salvation, is at the center of Augustine's vision of the future destiny of mankind. As for Tertullian—indeed, more so and far more profoundly so—the Greek concept of the soul is axiomatic. But by means of the personal struggle upon which he reflected in the *Confessions* and of the struggle to understand and explain the crisis of the Roman Empire and its relation to Christianity which is reflected in the *City of God*—not to mention the stormy conflict over the role of man in the achievement of salvation which he waged with the Pelagians—Augustine arrived at the new formulation of the vision of man's destiny based upon the impotence of man to control his unruly will.

The problem of the destiny of the soul between death and doomsday, for example, is treated very cautiously in the conclusion quoted above. The matter of the nature of the "secret shelter" for the soul is one concerning which speculation is essentially fruitless. If it is to be treated, however, the consideration must begin with the problem of the will, or, in the language of the creed, the "forgiveness of sins." Paul had said in I Corinthians 3:10-14 that one must live and work like a builder whose foundation is Christ and whose superstructure he knows will be tested by fire at judgment: even though the edifice may survive, the baser building materials will burn. Just so, the poorer parts of the edifice of one's life will be burnt away. Augustine treats this text, which was to become the chief proof text for the later doctrine of purgatory, as an allegory of life in the world. One builds wrongly, and therefore suffers chastisement as though by fire, in a manner directly proportional to the degree to which his will has been conformed to that of God. Such suffering serves to prepare the elect for their salvation: "He 'burns' with grief, for the things he has loved and lost, but this does not subvert nor consume him, secured as he is by the stability and indestructibility of [Christ] his foundation." [16] It is conceivable that such corrective punishment might continue after death, but this is essentially a matter of indifference to Augustine.[17]

Augustine is primarily concerned not with the individual in isolation but as a citizen of one of the unalterably and eternally opposed cities. The resurrection and judgment will stabilize the relationship of these and set eternally their boundaries. That is to say that those who by grace have brought their sinful wills under subjection will enjoy the vision of God while the other division of humanity will suffer "death eternal." This is the focal point of Augustine's teaching about the post-mortem destiny of man. It has a judicial element, but it is hardly so crude as in Tertullian, for Augustine's understanding is tempered by his conception of the depravity of the human will so that it becomes a marvel of grace that any man should be saved. There is no room for the almost gleeful vindictiveness of a Tertullian in this scheme. Damnation is "estrangement from the life of God," a fate all the more poignant because of the powerlessness of the unaided will to bring about a reconciliation with the God against whom it has rebelled. Augustine does not need to draw dreadful pictures of hell-fire and torment for anyone who can appreciate the horror of this eternal "exile."

The genius of Augustine's understanding of death resides in its unique marriage of the Latin and Hebrew concerns for history and justice with the detachment of the philosophical approach with its richly metaphorical possibilities. The synthesis achieved is immensely significant—and enormously difficult—precisely because of its balance of these two elements. Next to it, the metaphysical extremism of Origen and the religious rigorism of Tertullian tend to become caricatures, and nothing that had gone before (at least to the Western mind) even approaches a satisfactory solution to the problems raised by the confrontation of the Greek idea of immortality with the Judaic concept of raised or restored humanity. But the achievement of Augustine was based upon a careful balance and subtle distinctions which were difficult for lesser men to maintain. Athough all Western theology after Augustine was aware of his significance, few theologians understood his profundity.

GREGORY THE GREAT

One of the great mediators of Augustinian theology was Gregory the Great, a pope at the end of the sixth century, who may be regarded either as the last of the Romans or as the first medieval man. Among Gregory's most popular works is the *Dialogues,* in which he treats at the end of the destiny of the soul after its separation from the body in such a manner that he has been considered the originator of the Western Church's doctrine of purgatory.[18] Although *Dialogues* is classical in its form and in its attitudes, many of its passages introduce literary forms, not met heretofore in this survey, which will be of great importance as we examine ideas of death in the Middle Ages.

The passage which follows is Gregory's response to deacon Peter's asking "if we have to believe in a cleansing fire after death."

In the Gospel our Lord says, "Finish your journey while you still have light" [John 12:35]. And in the words of the Prophet He declares, "In an acceptable time I have heard thee, and in the day of salvation I have helped thee" [Isaiah 49:8]. . . . From these quotations it is clear that each one will be presented to the Judge exactly as he was when he departed from this life. Yet, there must be a cleansing fire before judgment, because of some minor faults that may remain to be purged away. Does not Christ, the Truth, say that if anyone blasphemes against the Holy Spirit he shall not be forgiven "either in this world or in the world to come" [Matt. 12:32]? From this statement we learn that some sins can be forgiven in this world and some in the world to come. For, if forgiveness is refused for a particular sin, we conclude logically that it is granted for others. This must apply, as I said, to slight transgressions, such as persistent idle talking, immoderate laughter, or blame in the care of property, which can scarcely be administered without fault even by those who know the faults to be avoided, or errors due to ignorance in matters of no great importance. All these faults are troublesome for the soul after death if they are not forgiven while one is still alive. For, when St. Paul says that Christ is the foundation, he adds: "But on this foundation different men will build in gold, silver, precious stones, wood, grass, or straw . . . and fire will test the quality of each man's workmanship. He will receive a reward, if the building he had added on stands firm! if it is burnt up, he will be the loser; and yet he himself will be saved, though only as men are saved by passing through fire" [I Cor. 3:12-15].[19]

The *Dialogues* is Gregory's response to the request of Peter and other members of the papal household for an account of the miracles of the Italian saints. Peter is said to have begged for such a work when Gregory complained that, under the burdens of his papal duties, he was unable to experience the joys of the contemplative life.[20] By the contemplative life, Gregory means the monastic life of withdrawal from the cares of the world. The monastic movement in Christianity had begun almost immediately after the recognition of the church by the Empire as, among other things, a means of accommodating those who wished to lead a rigorous or ascetic life in a world where martyrdom was no longer the end of rigorism. Earlier Fathers—Gregory of Nyssa and Augustine are notable among them—were sympathetic to monasticism and contributed to its development and institutionalization. But it was not until the age of Pope Gregory I that monasticism began to color general Christian piety and to offer an exceptionally attractive form of stable life of withdrawal from a civilization in a state of virtual collapse. Gregory was not alone in yearning for the security of the contemplative life, and his most significant contribution may be that he brought monastic thought and literary forms to the center of Christian intellectual concern.[21]

The present work is, in effect, a history of the Italian contemplatives and is composed primarily of accounts of their visions and miracles, which Gregory understood to be the fruits of ascetic or contemplative practice and which he regarded as providing glimpses of the ultimate reality. It begins with examples from the fairly remote past; book II is devoted to Benedict of Nursia (480-543), whose reputation as the father of Western monasticism is due in no small part to this treatment; most of the material of the third book is from the period 540-590. The final portion of the work contains some earlier examples, but it also uses exempla from his sermons and tales concerning members of his family;[22] in general it is concerned with contemporary events.

Yet, at the same time, as the fourth book of the *Dialogues* is a history of recent Italian asceticism, it is also a short essay on the immortality of the soul to confute those who doubt "that the soul will continue to live on after death." [23] An introduction arguing from Scripture demonstrates the survival of the soul (chapters 1-5); evidence is presented for the passage of souls at the moment of the body's death to an incorporeal state (chapters 6-25); a long section treats of the nature of the incorporeal existence of the soul (chapters 26-56); and the benefits of the mass offered as intercession are discussed in the conclusion (chapters 57-62). The experiences of contemplative men provide "experimental" support [24] for the initial arguments from scriptural authority.

Understood in its proper context, the passage under consideration adds nothing new to Christian teaching about death. Belief in the purgatorial effects of suffering during one's lifetime was, as has already been shown, a fairly constant element of theological discussion. Furthermore, the picture of a purification by fire at the time of the resurrection was a stock element of the apocalyptic tradition. Gregory does no more than continue the tentative suggestion of Augustine that this same kind of purificatory suffering might be an element of the adventure of the soul between death and resurrection. In a sense, Gregory is more cautious than his predecessor, for the passage ought probably to be read as saying, first, that there must be a purification for minor faults just before the judgment just as such purification can be a part of man's living experience, but that it is also possible that such purification will be experienced by the soul after its separation from the body. Gregory is, in other words, in essential agreement with Augustine on this point.

There is, however, even more which must be said about the views of Gregory and the context within which he presented his opinions. For example, it is clear that he believes that the political and social crisis of his own times presages the crisis of history, that the judgment is drawing near: ". . . in this land of ours the world is not merely announcing its end, it is pointing directly to it." [25] Thus, it is all the more imperative that men acquit themselves righteously. This belief introduces and frames *Dialogues,* IV. The destiny of the soul is considered in the light of the eschatological urgency. Furthermore, Gregory believes that the insights of the contemplatives into the nature of the future life are more clear precisely because the end is approaching. The present hour is like "the transitional hour before sunrise" when "darkness is somehow blended with light until the remaining shadows of the night are perfectly absorbed in the brightness of the coming day." [26]

Finally, the contemplative theme influences the presentation of the materials. The contemplative, for one thing, speaks by means of visions and dreams. Gregory has had a bad name for credulity in this regard,[27] but there is a sense in which the context of such visions and dreams is only the objectification of the doctrine of the journey of the soul which had been adopted by the Christian intellectual tradition from Platonism. What he says may be regarded as no more than graphic vindication of what the Fathers had generally taught about the soul. The monastic tradition had also tended to grant to the rigorous and contemplative ascetic the immediate entrance into Paradise which Tertullian and others had reserved for the martyrs. Gregory follows this tendency, and it is not always clear to his readers that when he speaks of the elect he means exemplary monks.[28] It is difficult for him to imagine—even for himself—that there may be exceptions to this rule.

Gregory the Great, then, maintains the general Latin patristic teaching about death, although the tone of his writing and the exaltation of the contemplative ideal tend to conceal the fact. The doctrine of the soul is axiomatic, and the pope believes that the soul will have some sort of disembodied active existence after its separation from the body. The nature of that existence remains undefined and is not really Gregory's chief concern. For the main thrust of God's judgmental activity—plentifully evident in present events—is reserved for the final judgment when body and soul will stand before God. Despite the strong influence of contemplative spirituality, traditionally Latin judgmental apocalypticism prevails.

The changes wrought on the biblical traditions regarding death in the patristic period were considerable. In no small degree those changes evolved because of the interplay between the Hebraic heritage of Christianity and the intellectual heritage of Plato in Greco-Roman civilization. Thus, the notion of resurrection and of the restoration of an elect people continued to be prominent. But the idea of a disembodied afterlife for the soul was also current and led to the conception of some sort of afterlife between the separation and the reunion of soul and body. From a picture of death as the inauguration of a sleep which would last until the divinely instituted resurrection, there emerged a picture of death as the beginning of a period of quiescence for the body and of a continued life for the soul, the nature of which remained more or less undefined. Greek theology tended to define that interim existence in terms of the metaphysical implications of the philosophical tradition. Latin theology viewed the same period in the light of the strong Roman belief that history is a struggle of moral against evil forces which eventuated in the judgment of men and their societies.

The remarkable fact about this course of events is that the chief emphasis of Christian teaching about death remained on the corporate picture of resurrection. The picture of sleep which arose from the unitive view of man in Hebraic thought did not make sense in a world which viewed man as a composite of mortal body and immortal soul. But Christian theologians, with remarkably few exceptions, tenaciously held to their apocalyptic sense that victory over death resides ultimately in the hands of the God who would raise and judge all men in the fullness of his time.

5 THE EARLY MEDIEVAL TRADITION

NORMALLY, A SURVEY OF A TOPIC in intellectual history would omit the period between Augustine and Anselm or even Aquinas. That practice is never defensible, and in this volume it is very important that reflections on death in the Early Middle Ages be considered in order to demonstrate that the pattern of teaching and opinion established in the Latin patristic writings was, in general, retained. The examples used to make this point will be drawn from England in the period before the Norman Conquest of 1066. This literature is not typical of the age in that, unlike writings from the Continent, which were almost exclusively in Latin, it is written in the Old English vernacular. However, the reader must accept the author's assurance that the English writing is based on Latin sources and in no regard deviates from the intellectual consensus and methodology of the continental writers. The center of intellectual life in Europe moved, after the decline of Rome, from the Mediterranean basin to the new Germanic kingdoms, and the English were always intimately connected with the new mainstream of theological and scholarly development.

Two marks characterize the theology of the period between Gregory the Great and the eleventh century. The first is a passion to collect, preserve, and transmit the teaching of the Fathers. However much one admires the achievements—even the innovations—of the scholars of this age, he must recognize the conservative temper of the monks, who were its professionally learned persons. The task of the scholar was to assemble the authoritative statements of the past on the subjects in which he was interested and to pass them on to future generations. Often his ability to assess the value of his sources was primitive, but the only measure he had for determining orthodoxy was authority: the authority vouched by the reputed sanctity of an author or supposed author.[1]

The second mark of the theological atmosphere of the Early Middle Ages is what has been characterized as the heroic outlook. In this remarkably unsettled period, high value was placed on personal ties of loyalty and on the ability of the strong lord to provide his retainers with security and the necessities of life in return for their own service and loyalty. So, analogously, Christ was regarded as the lord and hero *par excellence,* unremitting in his demand of obedience, who overcame Satan's power and his claims over the loyal Christian retainer. He had triumphed over death and one day would preside, as did the earthly lord in his hall, over the eternal and blissful banquet of his chosen and faithful followers.[2]

Both of these characteristics must be kept in mind as one examines the Old English literature, and one further feature which affects the selection of material for discussion must be mentioned. The works analyzed heretofore belong clearly to the classification of theology. This is not to say that there were not other forms of Christian literature in the patristic period. There is some verse which belongs both to the classical and Christian traditions; there is biography; there is a large, but often heterodox, visionary literature. All of these kinds of writing have a role in the history of the Christian intellect and imagination; but their relation to the history of classical thought and letters is such that, short of immensely complicating this study, it has seemed best to exclude them. The period from the end of the patristic age to the rise of scholasticism, however, serves as a funnel through which all these traditions were passed by the monks who were the sole preservers and practitioners of the literary arts. Hereafter (at least so far as this survey is to go) Western literature is assimilated into the Christian intellectual tradition, and can be treated as an integral part of it. Pieces which we would segregate from theology as *belles lettres* or as secular work were written in a historical context in which they were quite as much part of the undertakings of the Christian intellect and imagination as were exercises in dogmatic theology.

THE PHOENIX

The Fathers from very early times found the mythological phoenix of the classical tradition a convenient symbol of the resurrection;[3] indeed, not doubting the existence of the bird and believing that the phoenix was mentioned in Scripture, they regarded the case of the phoenix as a natural analogy to the resurrection.[4] One of the most interesting treatments of the phoenix motif is an Old English poem which was probably written in the ninth century.

In *The Phoenix,* a fourth-century Latin poem of Lactantius was adapted to provide an account of the bird. The poet then proceeded to meditate upon the phoenix's experience, applying it in turn to human life, to man's resurrection and subsequent heavenly dwelling, and, finally, to Christ. It is the transition from the first to the second of these applications which is of interest here: [5]

The righteous man earns eternal bliss, a heavenly home with the Most High [by pleasing God during his life], until the end of his days when death, murderous and armed warrior, snatches the life of every man and quickly sends transitory bodies deprived of souls into earth's bosom, where they will remain, covered by ground, until the coming of the fire.

Then all mankind will be led to the assembly; the Father of angels, true King of victory intends to hold a synod, the Lord of hosts to judge with equity. Then the resurrection of all men on earth will be accomplished, as the great King, Lord of angels and Saviour of souls, shall proclaim by the sound of the trumpet over the wide world. Dark death will be ended for the righteous by the power of the Lord. The noble will move about, the throng press forward when this world, sinful in its dishonor, burns, kindled by fire. Everyone will be afraid in his heart when the fire destroys the transitory riches of the world; the fire will utterly consume earth's riches, rapaciously grasp streaked gold, greedily swallow the fruits of the earth. Then in that time of revelation shall the fair and joyous significance of this bird [*i.e.*, the phoenix] come into the light; then the divine power will raise up all men, will gather bones from the graves, the body, limbs, and spirit of life together before Christ's knee. The King, gorgeous jewel of glory, will shine magnificently upon the holy from his high throne. It will be well for those who are able to please God in that sorrowful hour.[6]

The Phoenix is so complex and carefully wrought a poem that it is difficult and probably unfair to isolate a passage to make a point concerning the history of doctrine. Its parts are carefully knit together by the interplay of clusters of images. Thus, for example, in the portion of the poem based on Lactantius, there are passages reflecting Egyptian sun worship and the original setting of the phoenix myth. The sun is five times referred to as a "gem," [7] and the image is recapitulated and made to refer specifically to God in the picture of the day of resurrection. The images of the sun or God as a shining gem are only part of a larger complex of light images. This intricate but coherent technique gives the poem, which might in less-skilled hands have lost cohesiveness, a remarkable unity of tone and content.

The *Phoenix*-poet is clearly well-read in patristic literature and conversant with the doctrine of the soul. Death in the lines quoted is explicitly defined as the separation of body and soul. Resurrection is their reunion, and God is the Creator of souls. Yet, at least in the framework of these verses, the writer is not called upon to specify the nature of his understanding of the doctrine of the soul. One quite simple explanation of this phenomenon is the fact that the tradition makes the phoenix the symbol of resurrection and not of immortality.

But the explanation for the poet's comparative lack of interest in the doctrine of the soul is somewhat more difficult. At bottom, the answer to this riddle is probably the cultural one. Starting from a Latin poem dealing with the myth of the phoenix and incorporating what might be called the patristic phoenix-*topos* or stock interpretation of the myth,[8] the poet has achieved a synthesis, the balance and originality of which can only be explained in terms of his cultural ideals. His very opening sentences, which expound a single line in Lactantius, evoke not Egypt but the North of *Beowulf* and of Germanic legend.[9] Throughout the piece, the juxtaposition of classical source with the formulae of the northern epic poetry is striking.

The matter goes beyond language and tone to world-view, however. Reference has already been made to the so-called "heroic outlook" of early medieval theology. It pervades this poem, in which God is conceived very much as the Germanic chieftain who gathers about him those who do his will, distributing to them generous gifts, and who sternly punishes those who do not meet his standards. It can be argued very persuasively that in this cultural milieu the social conception of the last and everlasting great assembly of the King and Creator was more meaningful and appealing than more individualistic contemplation of the fate of the single soul. In other Old English poems, notably *The Seafarer* and *The Wanderer*, a man without a lord is portrayed as the archetype of human destitution whose only hope is that he will be accepted by God as one of his band of retainers. At any rate, our poet's picture of death is one of the beginning of a period of inactivity which will last until the call is sounded for the judgment.

Structurally, the passage under examination is a transition between a moral application of the phoenix story to man's earthly life and an analogy between the relation of the sun to the phoenix and of God to the elect.[10] Thus, the picture of the resurrection must be understood as a depiction of the fulfillment of life. The phoenix takes great pains to build his nest in paradise, his homeland, so that after his immolation and resurrection he will have a suitable dwelling. Man left paradise because of sin, but now he may regain paradise through the promise of resurrection. So almsgiving and other heroic deeds of the Christian life are the building of a nest, of a heavenly dwelling.[11]

Whatever the poet's conception of the soul may have been, therefore, and however he might have emphasized it in some other context, it seems clear that his primary hope is not for the soul but for the raised and reunified body and soul. The heroic picture of the judgment scene, of the court of the gift-giving King of kings, speaks to the Old English poet of his salvation. Thus, death, defined in the Hellenistic manner as separation of body and soul, was in fact a respite before the final reward or punishment.

SOUL AND BODY

This conclusion seems to be confirmed by other poems and prose pieces in which the soul occupies the center of the stage. An example of this literature is a poem which appears in the same manuscript, the Exeter Book, as *The Phoenix*. Known usually as *Soul and Body,* the piece consists of an address of the damned soul to its body which it revisits weekly for three hundred years after their separation.[12] The *topos* as it appears here represents a stage of development of a tradition which was ultimately based on the apocryphal *Vision of St. Paul*[13] and which continued to be influential in medieval literature as late as Dante.

Therefore it were far better for you [the Soul concludes its address to the Body] than that all worldly fortune were yours (except you had given it to God) that you had been created a bird or a fish in the sea, or toiled for food as a beast of the earth, as cattle roaming over the land without intelligence, yea! the fiercest of wild animals in the desert, had God willed, or that you were the most evil of the race of worms, than that ever you were a man in the world, or that ever you should have received baptism.

Then, at the great day, you will have to answer for us both when the wounds of all men are revealed which sinful men wrought of old in the world; then the Lord himself wants to hear of deeds, speech of the mouth from every single man, compensation for wounds. But what will you say to the Lord there on Doomsday? There will there be no joint too small on a bodily member that for each one separately you won't have to pay up the reckoning; the Lord at judgment will be severe. And what will we two do when he has raised us for another life-journey? Together we shall thereafter partake of such misery as you formerly prescribed for the two of us.[14]

In a number of ways the *Soul and Body* verses are closer than those of *The Phoenix* to the Latin tradition. Their diction is more like that of Latin or English homiletic prose than heroic verse. There is not so striking an effort as in the poem previously discussed to germanize the sources or the ideas. Indeed, this poem probably belongs to a slightly later time when men had become more used to adapting Latin prose to English and (through an inverse function of sophistication) had all but lost the creative gift of heroizing their Latin sources. The poem is related to the general soul-body *topos* which was used everywhere and by almost everyone in preaching repentance. It abounds in crudities, but they must be traced to the literary tradition and not to Anglo-Saxon primitivism. The description of the ravages of corruption in the grave, which follows the passage quoted, has a kind of vindictive and morbid "vigor" that makes "living flesh creep." [15]

In part, these matters of tone and taste may be excused if

one appreciates the purposes of the poem. It is a homiletic exercise designed to turn men from sin to virtue. As such, it must not be expected to reach the levels of profundity and sensitivity of an allegorical meditation such as *The Phoenix*. The longer version of the same poem, which appears in the Vercelli manuscript, has also an address of the blessed soul to its body; but it is weak in comparison with the speech of the wicked soul, for the dramatic and visual possibilities inherent in the excoriation of sinfulness are far greater.

The poem seems to assume that the soul has an afterlife in which its destiny is commensurate with the quality of its corporeal life. Curiously, it implies that it is the body which bears responsibility for the destiny of the soul. Thus, the soul's vindictiveness inspires a certain sympathy for the body in the reader. Death is the separation of soul and body; it inaugurates a period of awful decay for the body and of restless activity for the soul. Curiously, however, the soul is not really explicit about its own current mode of existence. Perhaps the poet (or his source) has been carried away by the temptation to describe bodily decay and forgotten the soul's fate. However that may be, the poem stresses not the torment of the soul, to which there are only fleeting allusions, but the body as food for worms. "Look where you are now!" is one focus of the soul's invective.

The other focus is, "See what will come!" The chief dramatic effect of the piece is prophetic; it points to doomsday and warns of the effects of sinfulness. The passage quoted above is, in other words, the climax of the poem. It is not simply the end of the soul's speech; it is the point to which the preceding invective was simply a prologue: the consummation of a life of sinfulness, whatever the horrors of the grave, is the great judgment. In the Vercelli version of the poem, the emphasis is the same; the coming judgment is a consolation which makes endurable, or is the vindication of, the ravages endured by the body in the grave.

Although it lacks a picture of the judgment itself, then, *Soul and Body* presents the same sort of configuration of events after death as *The Phoenix*. There is a doctrine of the soul, but it is undeveloped because the poet's interest is in the doctrine of resurrection. The metaphysical significance of the soul is forgotten or unrecognized. Even the rather limited kinds of speculation about the soul's independent existence which one finds in the Latin Fathers is lacking.[16] The Christian's hope has its fulfillment not in immortality but in resurrection and judgment.

AELFRIC OF EYNSHAM

The final early medieval document is a sermon by the most gifted Anglo-Saxon theologian after Bede—Aelfric, abbot of Eynsham, who wrote in the decades immediately preceding and following A.D. 1000. In Aelfric's work, I believe, one finds a higher level of theological sophistication than in either of the poems discussed above but a comparable general outlook.

Aelfric's great lifework was the preparation of a body of homilies in English to replace earlier collections of whose orthodoxy and accuracy he was dubious. Like the earlier homilists, but with a far more discerning eye and with a remarkable sensitivity to the possibilities of English prose, Aelfric's aim was simply to present useful material of unquestionable orthodoxy in easily understandable form. The successful pursuit of these aims was made possible by the labors of a generation of reformers of monastic life and study in England and on the Continent.[17]

The abbot of Eynsham's most extensive treatment of death is a long homily known in the manuscripts as *Sermo ad Populum in Octavis Pentecosten Dicendus*, or *A Sermon for the Laity for Delivery on the Sunday after Pentecost*. Some years before the piece was written, Aelfric had studied very closely a work by the late-seventh-century Spanish bishop, Julian of

Toledo, the *Prognosticon Futuri Saeculi (A Forecast of the Coming Age),*[18] and had himself written a Latin précis of it.[19] The English homily is based primarily on these excerpts from Julian; but new sources—especially from the Bible—were included, and the piece seems to have been prepared with considerable attention to detail.

The sermon begins with a résumé of the events commemorated by the church between Christmas and Pentecost that ends with an allusion to the theme of the Sunday after Pentecost, the worship of God in Trinity. The body of the homily deals with man's destiny from death through the judgment. It is not immediately clear why this subject suggested itself to Aelfric for the occasion, but it is possible that he wanted to spell out the implications for the individual of the events celebrated in the Christian calendar.[20] The topic is one which might have been brought to mind by the eschatological overtones of Ascension and Pentecost but for which there was no special provision in the Temporale.

The discussion of death and its aftermath seems to fall into three sections: death and the value of intercession, the condition of the soul after death and the day of Judgment.[21] Because it is our purpose here to assess the treatment of the soul's existence after death and that of the resurrection, it will be necessary to quote two passages. The first of these deals with the separated souls:

> God sends his angels to the death of good men, so that they might receive their souls at their death, and lead them to rest, as we learn in books, and Christ shows them their dwelling according to their merits. Those who are good and formerly pleased God in all good works will dwell with God; and those who are not very good, not entirely purged from all their sins, shall go to punishments and will suffer in punishments until they become clean and through intercession are released from thence. The wicked sinful ones who obeyed the devil in all their sins, and rejected their

Lord, and thus died, shall go to hell as soon as they die, and dwell there always. If the man should at least intend, when he is sick, to return to God and to confess his sins with true repentance, the just Judge will pardon him, so that he might at least on Doomsday escape the devil.[22]

The following is the concluding passage of the homily and the end of the description of the events of Doomsday:

Many of God's holy ones will come from earth to the heavens, for he wants to have a great band with him, as it well befits [him], and also they will be ordered each according to his merits, and further glorified with great glory as much as they, alive, loved their Creator; and there will be no envy among any of them, but they will all be in one concord and in true peace dwelling together. There he who was thought least dwelling in life will be very great and very famous in praise, and he will not desire any further glory beyond that which he will have through the gift of the Saviour. Everyone there will be able to see the thought of another man, he will never be hungry or troublesome, neither will thirst annoy him, nor will anything trouble him, but they all will be in one joy with Christ, loving him without intermission, and praising him without weariness, and Christ himself will then be all in all. He will be their power, and life, and glory, their salvation and glory, peace and abundance; and there will truly be one eternal day which will never end, and they then will be glorified twelvefold in soul and in body, and they will shine forever as brightly as the sun in their Father's kingdom. He who lives and reigns with his beloved Son and the Holy Spirit, in one Godhead, one almighty God, world without end. AMEN.[23]

The material of the first section of Aelfric's *Sermo ad Populum* displays no awareness of the philosophical issues; but it is derived from sources which considered the problem of eschatology in the light of the Graeco-Roman philosophical tradition. The death of the mortal body is unimportant in comparison with the destiny of the soul. For there are two deaths, that of the body, which all men must suffer, and that of the soul, which only the wicked endure and which is only metaphorically a death since it is more accurately described as the endurance of eternal punishment. To avoid this fate, it behooves us to lead a life acceptable to God and earn a place in heaven where a multitude of the saints already waits for us. If we are to win this goal, we need the prayers of the saints and the church. At the hour of death, God's angels come to judge the soul and lead it to heaven, to hell or to a condition in which it will be purged of its minor sins until released by expiation or by intercession. Sometimes, for those in the latter condition, a painful death serves the purpose of purgation.

The first passage quoted, dealing as it does with classes of souls and their existence in paradise, purgatory and hell, is far more systematic than anything seen before in this survey. It teaches unequivocally that the soul has an active future existence in a condition which is appropriate to the quality of its former life.[24] Here, then, there appears for the first time the kind of statement about the meaning of death usually associated with Western orthodoxy. The context emphasizes the efficacy of the prayers of the church in procuring the release of souls from temporary post-mortem punishment. Social contact between souls is said to be a feature of this incorporeal life.

Both the incorporeal punishment or reward and the social aspects of the soul's afterlife are made possible by the fact that "the soul has, truly, as books tell us, the likeness of the body in all its members, and it experiences comfort or pain. . . ."[25] Both in English and in Latin this statement betrays an original metaphysical doctrine of the nature of the soul, perhaps that of Tertullian. But even the author of Aelfric's source was probably unaware of the significance of such technicalities, and certainly the philosophical ramifications of the problem of the soul are the furthest thing from the abbot's mind. The teaching about the soul is something which he finds in old books of good authority. He accepts and reproduces it without question.

There is not space here to summarize the third and longest portion of Aelfric's sermon, in which he outlines the events of the final drama of salvation. It comprises more than half of the homily, and it inspires Aelfric to a generally higher level of eloquence and rhetorical display than do the earlier sections of the piece which, for Aelfric, are pedestrian. The treatment of the dramatic judgment parable of Matthew 25 is more complete than that of the sources and is a magnificent literary construction. Even the modernized version of the conclusion printed above gives some sense of the complexity of rhetorical structure and eloquence of tone. These facts suggest that Aelfric found the Doomsday scene more appealing and important than the picture of incorporeal afterlife. The spirit, if not the letter, is the same as that in the Old English poetry.

There is no escaping the fact that Aelfric, more clearly than any of the other theologians and poets discussed above, teaches that in the interim after death there is an active existence for the soul in which it suffers eternal or temporal punishment or enjoys eternal bliss until the fullness of time when "there are as many [just souls] as God ordained originally when he first created the whole world." [26] Like Augustine's and Pope Gregory's, Aelfric's teaching is closely tied to the practices of penance and of prayer for the dead. Unlike Gregory, the abbot of Eynsham does not rely on visionary materials to establish his case.[27] In part, the development reflected in the *Sermo ad Populum* is a side-product of the failure of the intellectuals of the Early Middle Ages to keep alive the philosophical tradition. Aelfric and his contemporaries were virtually illiterate philosophically. Immortality was unquestioned, but the ramifications of a doctrine of immortality were unrecognized.

But Aelfric was also prevented from developing his picture

of the afterlife by the very characteristics of theological method and the temperament of his age. The method of the age was encyclopedic: theologians gathered the wisdom of the giants of the intellectual heritage of the church. Finding little about the post-mortem condition of the soul in the authorities of the tradition, they had no tools with which to develop a new doctrine. Again and again, Aelfric cites old books as his sources, and, as often, he makes it clear that he has no intention of saying anything not vouched for by sound authority. Thus, had he wanted to, he could not have elaborated a new picture of the soul's future because to do so was beyond the very limited task set forth in the unquestioned understanding of the nature of theological method. Within a century after Aelfric's death, a new generation of scholars would instigate a "cultural revolution" by restoring logical studies to the curriculum.[28] When logical questions were asked of the materials of theology and when some awareness of other philosophical issues was manifested, the doctrine of immortality could be restated, and notions of the soul's afterlife might more easily be made an integral part of the theological system.

But it is equally important that the mentality or temperament of the times left theologians such as Aelfric disinclined to move toward a developed notion of purgatory or of the afterlife in general. For the heroic view of life was concerned with the individual as he took his place and played a role in the host of his lord, be that lord temporal or eternal. In the heroic age, the tragic figure was the man without a lord or companions. Thus, it was not the lot of the soul which preoccupied early medieval man but the destiny of the whole man: at the end, would he be at the table of the great Lord at his eternal banquet; or would he remain subject to Satan, the lord of darkness, who, but for the triumph of Christ, laid claim on all men? Given the doctrines of atonement implied by this set of values and attitudes, the doctrines of purgatory and of afterlife in the interim could never supplant the vivid picture of the heroic apocalypse in the imagination of theologian and layman alike.

Early medieval theology had in its classical and patristic heritage all the materials for a doctrine of purgatory and of an active spiritual afterlife. But the methodology and the mentality of the period prevented theologian and poet alike from seeing this fact and developing the doctrinal implications fully and logically. They remained peripheral and unarticulated. In a sense, the period is one in which one must report no development because the role of learning in the culture was to conserve rather than to innovate. In another sense, however, there is a development inherent in the very act of collecting materials and in adapting them to heroic, Germanic culture. Furthermore, these long centuries during which immortality went unquestioned as an integral Christian postulate made it easier, once the texts of the ancient philosophers had been recovered, to regard their teachings about the soul and its destiny as amplifications of the original gospel.

6 THE TRADITIONS OF THE HIGH MIDDLE AGES

THE HIGH MIDDLE AGES mark a turning point in the history of Christian thought concerning the meaning of death, for in this period the soul's immortality and its adventures after the separation of body and soul came to occupy the center of attention at the expense of the heroic picture of resurrection.

The revival of the study of logic has already been mentioned as an important factor contributing to this transformation. With logic as the basic methodological tool of the theologian and his ultimate criterion for determining the authority of any notion, the theological corpus underwent a radical revision. For example, the earlier age had explained salvation or atonement by reference to the descent into hell. In the harrowing of hell, Christ overcame Satan in a titanic cosmic struggle and thereby enabled his followers to elect a new allegiance to himself. Man was freed from an evil hero-lord to serve a just hero-lord. But the later theologians had found the notion that fallen man belongs by right to Satan distinctly unpalatable. Anselm, in *Cur Deus Homo,* overthrew this notion and substituted for it the explanation that God's justice demanded of man a satisfaction for sin so great that man was unable to pay. Therefore, God himself had become man to satisfy the demands of his own justice. Quite conscious of the radicalism of what he was doing, Anselm overthrew the heroic atonement for a new, more logical picture based upon the feudal understanding of legal obligations. The authority of hoary tradition no longer made for good theology. Logic was offended by a system which sees man as appropriately belonging to Satan, and, by using logically a new social analogy, theology could devise a new understanding of the role of Christ in man's salvation.[1]

Concurrent with this development, there emerged a generally different outlook on life which placed far greater emphasis than did the heroic on the individual, the character of his life, and his emotions. The tone of Christian piety was transformed. There is a new introspectiveness and a new desire for knowledge of self. The individual's worthiness to receive salvation is given a new stress in which his scrupulous satisfaction of the demands of divine justice came to the foreground and influenced a shift in emphasis from cosmic to individual salvation. At the same time, a new sense of tenderness, typified in theology by the cult of the Virgin and in letters by the courtly romance, coincided with a new means of formulating the quest or pilgrimage of the soul in search of perfection. The cosmic goal of the Kingdom of God remained, but judgment was set individually and at the hour of death.[2]

Perhaps, before turning to the theologian, this point could be documented in a preliminary way by reference to a thirteenth-century descendant of the *Soul and Body* poem discussed in the preceding chapter. The twenty-two-line poem can be translated in its entirety:

> Now is a man hale and sound, and evil enters his mind; then someone sends for the priest who knows well how to lead him to Christ. After the priest has come, sudden Death has taken him. They thrust him into a foul piece of cloth and lay him by the vault. On the morrow, whether in North or South, they take that body and bear it forth; they dig him a pit or a stone tomb and lay therein the fickle bone.

Then the soul says to the body, "Alas that I ever came into you! You would not fast until noon on Friday, nor give alms on Saturday, nor go to church on Sunday, nor do Christian works. Were you never so proud of your complexion and famous for your color, you will still have to dwell in the earth, and worms will chew you up, and you will be despised by all who were dear to you here.[3]

This crude piece can hardly be regarded as a good example of the new spirituality, but it is evidence for a radical transformation of the purpose, if not the content, of the soul-body *topos.* It alters the obsession with the physical manifestations of death and decay so that this feature of the tradition no longer represents the fate of the body in the interim before resurrection. One has the feeling that death is indeed terminal so far as the body is concerned. The picture is, at first, not one of moldering in the grave but of death and burial: the body is put away. The speech of the soul is likewise stripped of its emphasis upon ultimate resurrection. In this new context, the soul is by implication concerned only with its present state, which was brought on by the body's sinfulness. The soul seems to confirm the viewpoint of the first stanza by picturing the ravages of the grave as the ultimate punishment of the body.

All this is not to say that the resurrection is utterly eclipsed or atrophied in later medieval thought. Rather, it assumes a secondary role; and in part this new role is dictated by a new discipline, a new piety, and the new dialectical method.

THOMAS AQUINAS

The work of Thomas Aquinas represents one of the great achievements of the new approach to theology. His *Summa Contra Gentiles,* written between 1258 and 1263, was intended to assist Christians as they faced Islam both as a missionary challenge in Spain and, through the Islamic commentators on Aristotle, an intellectual challenge at Paris and other universities.[4] Thomas's better known *Summa Theologiae* was incomplete at his death, and its eschatological articles were provided later by disciples, so *Contra Gentiles* is the most complete treatment of our subject available.

The following passage, which deals with the fate of the soul immediately after its separation from the body, ought to give some indication of the general tone of Thomas's work:

There is . . . in the order of fault and merit a harmony with the order of punishment and reward. But merit and fault are fitted to the body only through the soul, since there is essentially no merit or demerit except so far as a thing is voluntary. Therefore, both reward and punishment flow suitably from the soul to the body, but it does not belong to the soul by reason of the body. There is, therefore, no reason in the infliction of punishment or bestowal of reward why the souls should wait for the resumption of their bodies; rather, it seems more fitting that, since the souls had priority in the fault or merit, they have priority also in being punished or rewarded. . . .

Nonetheless, one must weigh the fact that in the case of the good there can be an obstacle to keep the souls from receiving their ultimate reward, which consists in the vision of God, right after their release from the body. To that vision no rational creature can be elevated unless it be thoroughly and entirely purified, since that vision exceeds the whole of the creature's natural powers. . . . But by sin the soul is unclean in its disordered union to inferior things. To be sure, the soul is purified from this uncleanness in this life by penance and the other sacraments, as was said above, but it does at times happen that such purification is not entirely perfected in this life; one remains a debtor for the punishment, whether by reason of some negligence, or business, or even because a man is overtaken by death. Nevertheless, he is not entirely cut off from his reward, because such things can happen without mortal sin, which alone takes away the charity to which the reward of eternal life is due. . . . They must, then, be purged after this life before they achieve the final reward. This purgation, of course, is made by punishments, just as in this life their purgation would have been completed by punishments which satisfy the debt; otherwise the negligent would be better off than the solicitous, if the punishment which they do not complete for their sins here need not be undergone in the future. Therefore, if the souls of the good have something capable of purgation in this world, they are held back from the achievement of their reward while they undergo cleansing punishments. And this is the reason we hold that there is a purgatory.[5]

The first characteristic which distinguishes Thomas's work from that of the early medieval theologians is his profound interest in the doctrine of the soul as a metaphysical problem. Indeed, the problem of the soul was one of the chief topics of debate in the thirteenth century. Thomas, working on the Aristotelian base, developed a doctrine "that the soul, as pure form, actualizes the body as its matter, and that the intellective soul contains in itself in an eminent degree all the perfections of the sensitive and vegetative souls, which it supplants in the embryo of the human being at the moment of its creation." [6] In a metaphysical context similar to that of his development of the doctrine of Transubstantiation, Aquinas considered at length the issues of the relation of soul and body after death and of the interim between death and resurrection. He accepted immortality as a fundamental Christian tenet; but, unlike the early medieval theologians, he was aware of the philosophical issues raised and treated them sensitively and extensively.

But, as is evident from the treatment of the problem of the soul's destiny after death in *Contra Gentiles,* theological issues were also profoundly involved. The subject of eschatology is treated in Book IV, which deals with salvation. Thomas believed that salvation is by grace alone. Thus, he treats the doctrines of Christ, the Holy Spirit, and the Trinity as loci of teaching about God's gracious or saving activity among men and turns to the sacraments, which he regards as "instruments . . . of a God who was made flesh and suffered," as "visible things" which "work out a spiritual salvation." [7] At the end, he discusses the Last Things, the consummation of the work of salvation.[8]

The organization of these final chapters is, at first glance, curious; for Aquinas deals immediately with the resurrection of the dead—that great stumbling block to the "Gentiles"—with objections to it and with the nature of the body which is to be raised. As Christ died for "the remission of sin . . . , the sacraments work in the power of Christ." Similarly, as Christ was raised to effect "our liberation from death" mankind will be raised at the end of history.[9] This resurrection, metaphysically conceived, is necessary since the soul "is the form of the body" and "it is . . . contrary to the nature of the soul to be without a body." [10] Resurrection is also necessary in the light of "the natural desire of man to tend to happiness." Since perfect happiness is impossible in this world and impossible as well for the disembodied soul (for in that state it is imperfect), perfect happiness must await a future state in which body and soul will be reunited.[11] The same can be said in the light of the necessity that men be punished for their sins: ultimate punishment, like ultimate reward, demands reunion of soul and body.[12] In his risen and glorified state, or in his damned state, man will be immortal, animal, and incorruptible.[13] The effect of Thomas's treatment of resurrection is to make it absolutely clear that he takes very seriously the biblical texts upon which it is based and is intent upon interpreting those texts in a clear and logical metaphysical context. He is also concerned to fortify the biblical notions that Christ's sacrifice is an act of God's justice and that, without grace, man cannot be saved.

These latter considerations also motivate the treatment of the fate of the soul between death and resurrection. Punishment and reward are of the essence of God's justice, he asserts in the passage quoted above. One further element also argues for this conclusion: the soul as the rational element in man can have a vision of the divine once it is separated from the corruptible body; and, since that vision is "man's ultimate beatitude, which is the 'reward of virtue,'" punishment or reward is ineluctably the lot of the soul immediately after it is separated from the body.[14]

But the soul that is ultimately to be rewarded must be "entirely purified." Purgatory, in other words, is made necessary in the Thomistic system by the sacramental understanding of penance. In the sacrament of penance, the minister acts for Christ as judge of the sinner who is contrite for sins he has committed after baptism and imposes upon the penitent an obligation or "satisfaction." "By this a man is entirely freed from the guilt of punishment when he pays the penalty which he owed." [15] As further justification for the doctrine of purgatory, Aquinas cites the church's custom of praying for the dead,[16] but one has the impression that this argument is traditional and not so important to his position as it had been to the Latin Fathers.

After a passage in which he heightens interest in the state of the soul by arguing that the wills of souls separated from the body are immutable,[17] Aquinas finally considers the Last Judgment. There is, he declares, "a twofold retribution for what a man does in life"; one occurs for the soul immediately it is separated from the body, and the other will take place when the soul is reunited with its body. There is individual judgment at death, and there is general judgment at the end.[18] Metaphysically, since the soul is the form of the body and incomplete without the body, the Last Judgment is necessary. Practically speaking, the apocalypse is only the ratification of the judgment of the soul at the hour of death.[19]

Thus, Thomas Aquinas takes the biblical doctrine of the

resurrection of the dead very seriously and, at the same time, integrates that element of the church's teaching with the immortality of the soul in a metaphysically more satisfactory manner than even the great Greek Fathers. But this very success is one of the signs of a profound alteration of theological emphasis. For Thomas and his contemporaries were unwilling to leave unanswered, or as a matter of mystery, the question of the soul's fate between death and resurrection. They were impelled to ask what immortality means in the Christian scheme. Their answer was that the soul is judged at the hour of its separation from the body and enters immediately into its reward or punishment. The answer was not exactly a new one; it had been implied by the Fathers and stated by early medieval theologians. But it was pursued to its logical ends and given a new force and cogency in the High Middle Ages. The Last Judgment becomes a ratification of individual judgment. It represents the consummation of salvation and the goal of history, but it has lost its force as the focus of eschatological concern and primary element in the explanation of the meaning of death.

The very organization of Thomas's treatment at the end of the *Summa Contra Gentiles* demonstrates this phenomenon. The convincing and extended metaphysical case for the necessity of resurrection based on the notion that the soul is the form of the body is followed by a discussion of the soul's destiny before the resurrection. The reader's interest in this subject has been whetted by the important role played by the doctrines of the soul and immortality in the earlier books of this *Summa* and in the entire Thomistic corpus. Thomas's concern for this aspect of the history of the individual thus undercuts his concern with the dénouement of the history of mankind. And the two brief concluding chapters on the Last Judgment do not serve to restore the reader's interest in that event. It is, indeed, the consummation; but somehow, since the souls of those saved by the grace of God have already achieved the beatific vision, the coming of the end has lost its urgency and its place as the event for which the whole of creation yearns.

The increased importance of purgatory in this whole scheme only intensifies this development. If salvation is by grace, and if the sacraments are the chief vehicles of grace, then satisfaction or punishment imposed after priestly judgment and absolution becomes a vital element. Those who have not been purged while living must not be consigned to eternal punishment but must, in their disembodied state, be allowed to complete their satisfaction. At the time Aelfric wrote, while the sacrament of penance was certainly emerging, it had not yet reached its fully articulated form.[20] By the thirteenth century, penance was a vital element in the understanding of the justice and mercy of God. Thus, purgatory, as the state in which God graciously allowed one to complete his purgation, became increasingly important; and the tendency to view the existence of the soul in the interim after death as an active one was enhanced. Sacramentalism and the new interest in philosophical issues concerning the soul gave rise to an entirely new configuration of eschatological expectations.

DANTE ALIGHIERI

The *Divine Comedy* is an allegorical vision, the basic structure of which assumes the picture of the soul's destiny as it was painted by Thomas and his scholastic colleagues.[21] Although the dissemination of the scholastic view of the soul and the cosmos was certainly not the poet's primary purpose, Dante's role in its popularization in later ages has been considerable.

In the "Purgatorio," Dante and his guide, the pagan epic poet Virgil, are joined by the first-century poet Statius. Dante and his contemporaries regarded Statius as a Christian; thus, he is discovered in Purgatory, where he has completed his purification and can accompany Dante on his ascent to Paradise. As the three poets pass the cornice of the Mount of Purgatory reserved for the gluttonous, Dante observes that the souls suffering there are thin. His desire to know how the bodiless soul can be afflicted in this way is so great that Virgil tells him to loose the taut bow of his desire to speak. Virgil himself attempts to answer the question "How can souls grow thin?" by giving an example from mythology and an analogy based on form and its image in a mirror,[22] but he defers for a definitive answer to Statius. The "Christian" poet accepts this offer because Virgil asks, even though to do so he must "explain eternal things" in the presence of the pagan.[23]

Statius' disquisition opens with an account of the generation, embryonic development and creation of the individual soul,[24] which serves as a prolegomenon to his understanding of the nature of the soul's life after death:

> Then when Lachesis' flax is drawn, it frees
> itself from flesh, but takes with it the essence
> of its divine and human faculties—
>
> its lower powers grown passive now and mute;
> but memory, intelligence, and will
> more active than they were, and more acute.
>
> Miraculously then, by its own will,
> it falls at once to one or the other shore.
> There it first learns its way, for good or ill.
>
> And once inclosed in that new atmosphere,
> the *formative power* rays out, as it did first
> in shaping the bodily parts it left back there.
>
> Then, as the air after a rain will glow
> inside itself, reflecting an outer ray,
> and clothe itself in many colors—so

wherever the soul may stop in its new hour,
the air about it takes on that soul's image.
Such is the virtue of the *formative power.*

Thereafter, in the same way one may see
flame follow fire wherever it may shift,
the new form follows the soul eternally.

From air it draws its visibility. Hence,
it is called a *shade.* And out of air it forms
the organs of sight, speech, and every sense.

Thus are we able to speak and laugh. And thus
are we able to weep such tears and breathe such sighs
as you have seen and heard, passing among us.

As desire, or other feelings move us, so
our shades change their appearances. And that
is that cause of what amazed you just below.[25]

The first part of Statius' teaching deals with the coming together in the embryo of the vegetative, perceptive, and rational capacities to form the soul; it need not detain us. One of its primary purposes is to refute the supposed Averroist doctrine that the soul is mortal by asserting that the three capacities are fused by the gift of the divine spirit and made uniquely individual by virtue of that gift. By analogy, it is "as the sun's heat/joined to the sap of the vine turns into wine."[26]

When death frees this individuated soul, the "lower," or physical, functions are suppressed but the functions of the soul—"memory, intelligence, and will"—are intact and even enhanced. The separated soul "falls" straight away to hell, purgatory, or paradise. From its destination it knows its judgment, which is eternally fixed from the moment of death. In its new environment the soul's formative power works, as it had previously done in the formation of the embryo, to shape for the soul an incorporeal body. The nature of this body or shade or apparition—that which Dante sees on his journey—is to be understood by means of analogy with the rainbow, which is the appearance of color in the atmosphere caused by the concurrent presence of the sun's rays and moisture. As the rainbow is visible, so the image of the soul is visible in the "atmosphere" of the other world by virtue of the power of the ray, or formative virtue of the soul. This manner of conceiving the nature of the soul's existence is not one held in common by Dante and the Thomists, for the latter do not go on from their exposition of the nature of the incorporeal life to posit an effect on the atmosphere which produces the shade. For Thomas the incorporeal soul is formless. This device is one which enables Dante to emulate Virgil's underworld; but it is surely not simply a poetic device, for it seems to restate a position the poet had taken in earlier works.[27]

Whereas the body was mortal and corporeal, this form is incorporeal and immortal. The shade, Statius concludes, has all the faculties of the body and can experience emotion or pain. So it is that the punishment of the gluttons consists of temptation with food and its concurrent denial, and that their shades become emaciated as a result of their starvation. In other words, Dante's shades are capable of experiencing in every way the punishments required by their earthly misdemeanors. In this view, based as it is upon the conceptualizations of contemporary intellectuals, the requitals of the disembodied afterlife are efficient and sufficient; the purgations of resurrection day are again redundant. The soul is both immortal and capable in its disembodied state of discharging its responsibilities for its worldly existence.

The resurrection as the goal of Christian existence is not utterly lost in Dante's scheme. It is scriptural, it involves reunion of body and soul, and it is the object of the theological virtue of hope.[28] Near the beginning of the *Inferno,* it is said that the soul will return to its body at the sound of the trumpet to hear the eternal judgment. Since, so unified, man more nearly approaches perfection, the more perfect are his sensations of pleasure and pain. The damned will suffer in a manner even more commensurate with their deserts than they do now.[29]

Passages such as these preserve in Dante the outline of the traditional Christian doctrine of resurrection. But again one feels that the focus of attention has shifted from the ultimate goal to the proximate destiny of man. Salvation is determined and judgment is effected for the soul at the moment of death, and the resurrection only reaffirms a fact. Life wins eternal salvation, eternal salvation after temporary purgation, or eternal damnation for man; and the individual soul has what it deserves without waiting either for his body or for the rest of mankind.

Although the emphasis on the education of the soul in Dante's discussion is more significant and more carefully developed than in any of the writings surveyed here except those of Origen, Dante avoids the abstractness and gnostic tendencies of Origen and even the perils of overintellectualization inherent—or at least potentially present—in Thomas Aquinas. This is due not simply to his powers of portrayal but to his sense of the historical and to his genius for understanding that man's historical manner of life prefigures his eternal manner of life. Judgment, in other words, is a function of history.

Dante shares this precept with his contemporaries, but his poetic gift appropriates it in such a way as to transcend all rivals. Thus, the vision of the *Comedy* is only the best example of a vital fact which a survey like this might well overlook. While the point of central interest in reflection on the significance of death shifted in the High Middle Ages from resurrection to the soul's immediate post-mortem fate, the medieval doctrine of the soul differed radically from the Greek and

Hellenistic in that it took very seriously the importance of existence in history, the uniqueness of one's historical experience and the once-for-all judgment of that historical being. "The human world in all its breadth and depth is gathered into the structure of the hereafter and there it stands: complete, unfalsified, yet encompassed in an eternal order. . . ." [30]

WILLIAM LANGLAND

It needs, finally, to be pointed out that the heroic and apocalyptic tradition of the Early Middle Ages persisted into and beyond the age of Aquinas and Dante, and that the schoolmen and those whom they influenced did not consider it inconsistent with their own system. One might look to monasticism, to certain strains of popular piety, or to aspects of the mystical tradition for evidence of the persistence of this approach to the problem of death, but perhaps it can best be seen in the great vision of William Langland, the late-fourteenth-century English poet. This vision is generally called *Piers Plowman*. Like the *Divine Comedy, Piers Plowman* is a poem about the perfection of man through the Christian way of life; but, whereas Dante approaches his subject by portraying man's ultimate destiny against which his present life must be measured, Langland depicts the quest of perfection in the world.[31]

The following passage is part of Langland's dreamer-narrator's rather intemperate response to the comments of Scripture, whom he had asked how to achieve perfection. Instead of directions, Will complains, he received a lesson in theology. He may have the schoolmen in mind when he asserts that many scholars gather knowledge as other men accumulate property but, at the end, find themselves bereft of grace. At any rate, that rather uncharitable view is illustrated by the following biblical examples:

But I suppose it will be of many [Christian teachers and

scholars] as it was in Noah's time when he made the ship of planks and boards: no carpenter or workman who worked on the ship was saved, only birds and beasts and the blessed Noah and his wife with his sons and also their wives; of the carpenters that wrought it, none was saved. God grant that it be not so for the folk who teach the faith of Holy Church, which is a harbor and God's house within which we are saved and shielded from sin as Noah's ship protected the beasts; and the men who made it drowned in the flood. . . . On Doomsday there shall be a flood of death and fire together; therefore, I counsel you clerks, the carpenters of Holy Church, do such deeds as you see prescribed in Scripture lest you not be within.

On Good Friday, I find, a thief who had lived all his life by lies and theft was saved; and because he confessed on the cross to Christ, he was saved sooner than Saint John the Baptist, and either Adam or Isaiah or any of the prophets who had lain with Lucifer many long years. A robber was released to eternal joy sooner than any of them without any penance in purgatory.[32]

Langland is actually unconcerned in his great poem with the phenomenon of death, the destiny of the soul, and the resurrection of the dead. Yet all three of these topics are implicit in Will's quest for perfection and in his apocalyptic sense of the urgency of that quest. In his opening vision—and, indeed, throughout the work—the world is pictured as a "fair field full of folk" which stands between a hill to the East topped by the tower of Truth and an abyss containing the dungeon of Falsehood.[33] The field represents life in the world with its manifold activities and classes of men. It is poised between heaven and hell, and life is a struggle to gain the one and to avoid the other.

Critics have sometimes claimed that the poem is characterized either by a prophetic desire to transform or by an ascetic yearning for spiritual perfection. The vision of the "field full of folk," however, precludes exclusive concern with either social reform or asceticism. Like the early medieval monks, Langland has a desire for perfection of the soul but is unable to divorce it from man's historical existence. Man, spiritual and historical, stands in the field between two awful opposing forces and struggles to attain the tower of Truth. Enlightenment and reform are, therefore, inseparable.[34]

The general ambiance of *Piers Plowman* probably explains the lack of concern with the destiny of the soul. The very symbols of the allegorical cosmos preclude a picture of the adventures of the soul, for life (the field) is poised between the two ultimate forces in such a way that the social and the spiritual cannot be separated and so that it becomes impossible for Langland to treat directly the suprahistorical. In the same way, although he deals with the descent of Christ into hell and the apocalyptic reign of Antichrist, Langland does not describe Doomsday because of his unique preoccupation with the present struggle of man.[35]

Neither purgatory—or the scholastic picture of the destiny of the soul—nor resurrection is denied by Langland. Indeed, the acceptance of both in the passage selected for treatment here is quite clear. The poet is aware of his contemporaries' philosophical discussions of the nature of the soul[36] and of the general view of afterlife. But his feelings about the urgency of life in the world are such that, unlike Thomas and Dante, he does not emphasize these elements of eschatology. If the Doomsday scene lies outside his artistic needs, however, it is clear that the older apocalyptic approach to the interpretation of death is closer than the scholastic to his own piety. His treatment of the work of Christ, especially in the great vision of the Harrowing of Hell in Passus XVIII is that of the old, heroic theology; and the tone of historical urgency and reiteration of divine judgment strongly color the entire work so that, even if the judgment scene is only incidentally described, its influence is felt on every page. At two crucial points when he deals with the nature of divine pardon or the achievement of perfection, he paraphrases the clause of the Athanasian Creed which describes the final judgment after the resurrection.[37]

The view of *Piers Plowman* is an old-fashioned one, more reminiscent of early medieval theology than of scholasticism. Although it does not counter the scholastic stress on the post-mortem journey of the soul, it nevertheless leaves little room for emphasis upon that theme but rather emphasizes both in tone and content the heroic and the apocalyptic in order to underline the importance of the quest for perfection in the midst of evil in the world.

The point seems at first ironic, for William Langland describes himself as a married man in lower orders who makes his living saying offices of intercession for the souls of the dead.[38] This fact seems, however, neither to have troubled Langland nor to have occurred to him. The poet's obliviousness was probably made possible by the trait of Langland's which most clearly distinguishes his work from that of the earlier Middle Ages: a highly individualized piety in which questions of conscience and psychology predominate. Langland was in this regard an intellectual descendant of Bernard of Clairvaux, whose formulation of the problem of the will permeates his work.[39] Within this "psychologized and interiorized" frame of reference and influenced by its emphasis on "the personal way to God and the importance of conscience," [40] Langland was able to deal either with the penitential system and its intercessory offices in his daily life or with the apocalyptic and historical tradition in his writings without perceiving the potential conflict between the two.

In *Piers Plowman,* then, we see the early medieval apocalyptic stress on resurrection and judgment continued but transformed by the new piety of the later period, which stressed personal destiny in terms of the judgment of the soul.

The three documents discussed in this chapter are very

different from each other and yet only partially reflect the great diversity of views of death in an age which was uniquely preoccupied with death.[41] Two of the most significant literary and theological themes of the period—contempt of the world *(contemptus mundi)* and the remembering of the fact of death *(memento mori)*—have had to be overlooked because they stress not so much the nature of death as the fact that it is the lot of every man. In all the arts, death tended to be intellectualized and individualized. As in the *summae* of Thomas, the decorative programs of the churches articulated a view of death which emphasized the destiny of the individual from death to Doomsday and which tended to stress judgment as simply the ratification of a process essentially complete at the moment of death. The great poetic vision of Dante demonstrates the same kind of development but also serves to underline the fact that the belief that history determines one's eternal lot was not abandoned when theology turned from the apocalyptic picture to a picture based on the Greek metaphysical concept of the journey of the soul. And Langland serves to remind us that the older heroic theology did not entirely disappear as a result of the triumph of logic and individualism.

In general, however, this period marks a significant change in the Christian view of death. Heretofore, theologians and poets had been satisfied to leave the riddle of the soul's fate between death and the judgment unanswered. Hope had been focused upon the resurrection. But new formulations and new questions led to the closing of the gap and to the portrayal in detail of the joy, the agony, or the temporary suffering of man's soul after death. The one pope of the period who suggested that the soul had to await the resurrection before entering a state of beatification or of damnation was severely criticized by the scholars of the universities and forced to retract on his deathbed.[42]

7 THE SIXTEENTH-CENTURY TRADITION

THE FOURTEENTH AND FIFTEENTH CENTURIES have often been regarded as the age during which the abuses inherent in the thirteenth-century social, intellectual, and theological "syntheses" ran rampant. It is true that feudalism was giving way to nationalism. It is apparently true that abuse was rife among some popular preachers and that superstition increased among the unlettered. It is true that the hierarchy tended to fix its views on indulgences as related to purgatory and that, among other things, at the Council of Florence in 1439 the papacy tried to impose the Western understanding of purgatory and afterlife upon the Greeks, who, in general, had maintained a position based on that of the Cappadocian Fathers.[1] But it is also becoming clear that this view of the character of the period is simplistic. It is unfair to speak of a triumphant synthesis in the thirteenth century; and it is now recognized that lively theological debate, which was necessary preparation for the Reformation debate, took place throughout the intervening period. The age was one of violent disagreement—even revolution—within Christendom; success against very great odds is one of the most remarkable features of the Reformation. As for superstition, it must not be confused with the long tradition of apocryphal, visionary, apocalyptic literature which had been popular from earliest times and had produced some of the greatest Christian imaginative literature: we have seen that tradition in Pope Gregory I and the Saxon homilists; it had its most sublime expression (joined with the scholastic learning) in the *Divine Comedy* of Dante; it continued in a more primitive form in the work of Langland.

Several scholars [2] have recently pointed to a new conclusion about the nature of late medieval theology and have shown that the period was characterized by ongoing debates concerning the doctrines of justification, authority, and the church. It begins to appear that future generations will understand the sixteenth century as the last phase of medieval intellectual history and the seventeenth as the beginning of a new era. It is, at any rate, in this light that I believe we must regard the reformers' attitude on the problems of purgatory and immortality; and, to establish my point, I should like to look to Luther, to Calvin, and to Shakespeare's *Hamlet*.

MARTIN LUTHER

The German reformer was once asked whether the Fathers taught anything about purgatory and, if so, which was first. The answer sounds rather as though it may have been an accepted opinion at the time:

> Luther replied that neither Ambrose, Augustine, nor Jerome thought anything about purgatory, but Gregory, deceived by visions, had taught something regarding purgatory, although God forbad that anything be tested by spirits rather than by Moses and the prophets. In this regard, therefore, nothing should be conceded to blessed Gregory. . . . God in his Word offers to us two ways: salvation through faith, damnation through unbelief. He makes no mention of purgatory. Purgatory is not to be admitted, because it obscures the merits and grace of Christ.[3]

Luther was probably thinking of Gregory's *Dialogues* when he made these comments. Whether or not this opinion was a commonplace of the schools before his time, it has become one since.

Nevertheless, this position is a rather stronger one than Luther had taken earlier in his career. He had not originally denied the existence of purgatory, but he wanted it admitted that the doctrine was a postbiblical one developed at a comparatively late stage. "It is enough," he declared in 1521, "to know that [the sinful dead] suffer great and unbearable pain and crave your help. But if you wish to discuss the question then you must leave room for surmise and differences of opinion, as I do." [4] Indeed, Luther's original attack on purgatory in the *Ninety-five Theses* of 1517 was directed not against the concept itself but against its close connection with the sacrament of penance and certain abuses in the use of indulgences to remit satisfactions adjudged by the temporal church.[5] As his thought developed—and as the events of the Reformation led him on—Luther's position against purgatory hardened. And this was reinforced by a growing skepticism about the value of prayers for the dead. One ought, he believed, to pray for the dead at the time of death, but repeated masses become "useless mummery" and must only annoy God as a sign of faithlessness, since whatever is asked believingly will be given.[6] As for the faithful departed, Luther did not challenge the view that they are "with God . . . in eternal blessedness"; [7] but neither did he indulge in speculative description of their condition.

Because of his adherence to the principle of *sola scriptura,* the eschatological notes in Luther's writings have a remarkably primitive flavor. The state of man in the interim after death is of little interest to him, although he often resorts to such stock patristic euphemisms as "Abraham's bosom." Furthermore, since Christians are baptized "into death" they have taken a first step in preparation for death; and "though they are baptized to eternal life in the Kingdom of God, they do not right away possess its fullness." [8] Life in this world is purgatory enough. So one must distinguish between "the separation of body and soul," which is "a symbol and a parable . . . like a picture of death painted on a wall," and "eternal death . . . by which the soul is freed and separated from sin and the body from corruption, and the soul is united by grace and glory with the living God." [9]

In part, Luther's lack of explicit interest in the question of immortality may also be due to his methodological principle, derived from late medieval philosophy, that philosophy has to do with reason and theology with faith. Thus, his attack on the overemphasis on Aristotle in the schools is based on his concern that theologians have misused the philosopher, taken him out of his field.[10] The criticism of Aristotle's *De Anima* for teaching "that the soul dies with the body" [11] is significant notice that Luther regards immortality as an essential element of good philosophy. But at the same time, it must be remembered that Luther wanted Aristotle's logical and rhetorical treatises (his methodological treatises) retained in the curricula.[12]

In other words, the attack on purgatory is part of the attack on the penitential system; and a position on the destiny of the soul is not worked out for methodological and exegetical reasons. Thus, it is difficult from a reading of Luther to come to clear conclusions as to his position on the afterlife. But there is sufficient reason to believe that Luther represents a continuation of medieval debates and opinions rather than an utter break with the immediate past.

JOHN CALVIN

Unlike Luther, most of whose works are occasional, John Calvin set out to write a system, or *summa,* of reformed theology in which, dealing with an astounding range of patristic and scholastic literature, he preserved the tradition of dialectic, which primarily characterizes medieval theology. The *Institutes of the Christian Religion* [13] is a debate with the tradition, and especially with the medieval tradition; and, therefore, it stands as much within the heritage as over against it. Indeed, the elaborations the work underwent as it grew from a comparatively small volume in its first edition of 1536 to its final, massive form in 1559 serve mainly to increase the scope of Calvin's dialogue with his predecessors and contemporaries. The fact that Augustine, after Paul, is Calvin's most compatible theological colleague only ties him to one of the two chief strands of medieval theological thought.

Calvin's treatment of the Last Things is integrated into Book III of the *Institutes,* rather as Aquinas's is concentrated in Book IV of *Summa Contra Gentiles*. Indeed, except for the fact that Calvin relegates his discussion of the Sacraments to Book IV as a subdivision of ecclesiastical polity, there are striking similarities in their treatments. Both consider eschatology under the heading of salvation; having treated the problem of the knowledge of God, they turn to his saving work.

The following passage is central to Calvin's argument concerning the nature of the afterlife:

> Now it is neither lawful nor expedient to inquire too curiously concerning our souls' intermediate state. Many torment themselves overmuch with disputing as to what place the souls occupy and whether or not they already enjoy heavenly glory. Yet it is foolish and rash to inquire concerning unknown matters more deeply than God permits us to know. Scripture goes no farther than to say that Christ is present with them, and receives them into paradise [cf. John 12:32] that they may obtain consolation, while the souls of the reprobate suffer such torments as they deserve. What teacher or master will reveal to us that which God has concealed? Concerning the place, it is no less foolish and futile to inquire, since we know that the soul does not have the same dimension as the body. The fact that the blessed gathering of saintly spirits is called "Abraham's bosom" [Luke 16:22] is enough to assure us of being received after this pilgrimage by

the common Father of the faithful, that he may share the fruit of his faith with us. Meanwhile, since Scripture everywhere bids us wait in expectation for Christ's coming, and defers until then the crown of glory, let us be content with the limits divinely set for us: namely, that the souls of the pious, having ended the toil of their warfare, enter into blessed rest, where in glad expectation they await the enjoyment of promised glory, and so all things are held in suspense until Christ the Redeemer appear. The lot of the reprobate is doubtless the same as that which Jude assigns to the devils: to be held in chains until they are dragged to the punishment appointed for them [Jude 6].[14]

The treatment of the problem of the afterlife begins for Calvin, as for Luther, with the consideration of purgatory and repentance. Calvin believes that repentance is the manner in which faith works to reorient man's life to God. Repentance is "regeneration, whose sole end is to restore in us the image of God that had been disfigured and all but obliterated through Adam's transgressions." [15] Thus understood, the mortifying and vivifying work of repentance must not be allowed to become an outward work, a chief end of Christian life.[16] For this reason, the whole rationale of sacramental penance is to be attacked. The penitential system serves only to drive man to desperation, because it does not "teach [man] in his humility to give glory to God." [17] This is not to say that confession is not a vital element of Christian life and ecclesiastical discipline,[18] but that scriptural and primitive practices have been perverted. It is the element of satisfaction in medieval theory which most distresses Calvin, for it is Christ who is the propitiation for the sins of the world.[19]

Thus, the whole system of indulgences and the doctrine of purgatory must be wiped out if the church is to return to a proper understanding of repentance. The notion of a treasury of merits, on which indulgences rest, is blasphemous, for it leaves "Christ only a name [and makes] him another common saintlet who can scarcely be distinguished in the throng." [20] Purgatory falls with indulgences and with the doctrine of satisfaction: ". . . if it is perfectly clear . . . that the blood of Christ is the sole satisfaction for the sins of believers, the sole expiation, the sole purgation, what remains but to say that purgatory is simply a dreadful blasphemy against Christ?" [21] The standard biblical proof texts are shown to refer to the fact that man undergoes tests in life.[22] The appeal to the custom of praying for the dead fails, for "the ancients" prayed "in memory of the dead" and "were in doubt concerning the state of the dead." [23]

So, for Calvin the medieval doctrine of purgatory is objectionable not because of its connection with the notions of immortality or of afterlife, but because it is a perversion of the tradition. It rests on a false, sacramentalized understanding of repentance and on the custom of prayers in memory of the dead. It is an abomination because it undercuts the sole ground of salvation: the sacrifice of Christ by whose merit alone the elect are redeemed. It is unnecessary and unthinkable.

What, then, of the problem of afterlife before the resurrection of the dead? In the first book of the *Institutes* in its final form, there is a lengthy discussion of the immortality of the soul, which is presented in connection with the doctrine of creation. It is, for Calvin, "beyond controversy" that "man consists of a soul and a body," that soul (or spirit) is immortal [24] and that the soul is in man "the proper seat" of the image of God.[25] While scripture teaches the immortality of the soul, the proper realm for discussion of the "faculties" of the soul is philosophy; and, among the philosophers, Plato is commended as a good teacher in this area of learning, which is "not only enjoyable, but also profitable." [26] These views are implied when—after disposing of false views of repentance and of purgatory—Calvin discusses the nature of Christian life in the world. A strong element of what Max Weber called the "worldly asceticism" of Calvin is "meditation on the future life," which is resignation to the fact that life in the world is "nothing but struggle" and concentration on the only hope: "heavenly immortality." [27] If there is a purgation, it is this present life. Thus, Calvin concludes, in terms which recall the stoicism of Cicero, the Latin literature of consolation, the asceticism of the monks, and the medieval contempt for the world, "in comparison with the immortality to come, let us despise this life and long to renounce it. . . ." [28] Although there are allusions in this passage to the Last Judgment, the major thrust—reinforced by commendation of the "contempt of death" in pagan philosophy—is to emphasize an immediately enjoyed immortality of the soul.[29]

Finally, after outlining his crucial doctrines of justification and election,[30] Calvin treats the resurrection. Bereft of a purgatory and of metaphysics, his analysis is yet very like that of Thomas. It begins with an assertion of the vital importance of the biblical doctrine and an analysis of the nature of the body to be raised; there is a refutation of false speculations about the nature of the glorified body.[31] At this juncture, Calvin inserts the passage previously quoted on the interim existence of the soul. It is not proper, he maintains, to "inquire too curiously concerning our souls' intermediate state" —"Abraham's bosom" is designation enough for the faithful— but it is clear that Calvin regards the state of the souls before the resurrection as an active one. Indeed, he is so vehemently opposed to Pope John XXII's heretical doctrine of the "sleep of souls" that he regards John's case as proof of the fallibility of the papacy.[32] Finally, Calvin describes the resurrection itself, the acceptance of the elect and the alienation of the reprobate.

In the consideration above of the comparable portion of the *Summa Contra Gentiles,* it was maintained that Thomas leaves the impression of being primarily interested in the interim destiny of the soul, of its individual judgment of which the general judgment is but a reaffirmation. I would argue that, although many mythological details (like the judgment of the separated soul) are missing in Calvin, he, too, betrays a greater concern with immortality than with the resurrection. For both theologians, the last state of man only perfects the condition of the elect and reprobate in the interim after death. Combined with the interest elsewhere in the *Institutes* in immortality and with the commendation of the teachings of Plato and other "philosophers" on this score, Calvin's treatment of eschatology betrays a greater concern for the interim blessedness or punishment of the soul than for its reunion with the body at the end of the age.

The reformers, then, attacked purgatory as a teaching inseparably connected with what they regarded as the most corrupt part of the medieval ecclesiastical system, the sacrament of penance. It was false to say that the temporal church can impose works of satisfaction which would continue after death. And it was dubious to argue by pointing to the ancient custom of praying for the dead that the souls of the dead suffered purgation from which the church might release them by prayer. But, unlike at least some of the Greek Fathers, the reformers did not see that the concept of immortality of the soul was not biblical but Greek. Thus, their claim to have reverted to the pure teaching of the Bible—or even of the Fathers—must be challenged. They stood directly in the tradition of the medieval churchmen who felt that an active interim existence for the soul was part and parcel of the basic Christian eschatology. Although Calvin left the details of the interim vague, as had the Fathers, the tone and emphasis are not those of the patristic period. The emphasis of teaching about eschatology remained in the sixteenth century, as in the Middle Ages, on the interim after death and not on the Last Judgment.

HAMLET'S GHOST AND THE ENGLISH REFORMATION

As C. S. Lewis pointed out some years ago, William Shakespeare's *Hamlet* might easily be read as a play about death or (more accurately) a play in which the hero, and therefore the audience, is kept thinking about *"being dead* . . . all the time." [33] Hamlet meditates upon the comparative disadvantages of being dead or alive: "To be or not to be. . . ." He hesitates when an opportunity presents itself to kill King Claudius at prayer because the king might be in a state of grace and avoid the torments he deserves (ironically, he is not). The priest makes a judgment on the state of the soul of Ophelia, who has killed herself. Hamlet considers the skull of the jester Yorick and comments on the decomposition of the body in the grave. All the themes of the medieval *memento mori* are touched upon as Hamlet meditates upon the fate of man after the hour of death. There is even the ghost, who reports, by employing the medieval rhetorical device known as *occupatio* or refusal to report, from beyond the grave:

> I am thy father's spirit
> Doom'd for a certain term to walk the night,
> And for the day confin'd to fast in fires,
> Till the foul crimes done in my days of nature
> Are burnt and purg'd away. But that I am forbid
> To tell the secrets of my prison house,
> I could a tale unfold whose lightest word
> Would harrow up thy soul, freeze thy young blood,
> Make thy two eyes, like stars, start from their spheres,
> Thy knotted and combined locks to part,
> And each particular hair to stand on end
> Like quills upon the fretful porpentine.
> But this eternal blazon must not be
> To ears of flesh and blood. . . .[34]

Historical accuracy of detail was never one of the goals of William Shakespeare's dramatic art. The household of Olivia in *Twelfth Night,* though the dramatic scene is "a city in Illyria," is clearly staffed and managed as were households of wealth and ease in Elizabethan England. The players in *Hamlet* arrive at the ancient seat of the Danish kings gossiping of the activities and controversies of English theatrical companies at the turn of the sixteenth and seventeenth centuries, and the prince himself is said to have attended a university founded in the sixteenth century and associated with Luther. Thus, one cannot dismiss the elder Hamlet's report of his soul's fate as an effort to reconstruct medieval doctrine.

Yet the playwright also attempted to avoid topicalism by setting his plays in distant, romantic lands or (notably in *Hamlet, Macbeth,* and *Lear*) by imparting a tone of primitivism and mysteriousness to plays set in the dusky, early days of Germanic Europe. Thus, it is difficult to know at what points the characters represent the author's point of view, particularly in matters touching on religious belief. The problem is made more difficult by the fact that so little is known about the sources Shakespeare used in shaping *Hamlet.*

Caution is, therefore, demanded of the reader who wants to draw conclusions for the history of religious thought from *Hamlet.* At most, one can remark on the materials Shakespeare presented to his audience as though they were common and current, ideas he does not seem to have thought would be regarded as controversial or derogatory of his characters. He may only have sought historical verism in his depiction of the scruples of a Catholic prince, but his Elizabethan audience and audiences ever since have not been shocked by his picture of death.

The ghost-king of *Hamlet* clearly intends to inform his son that he suffers in a state of purgation. At night, he may not rest but walks; during the day he is tormented by fire, and this state will endure until his sins have been atoned. His expression "foul crimes" apparently represents an interpretation from beyond the grave of the qualities of his life and reign; for the son and others remember him as a good king, albeit a manly man subject to normal frailties. In any case, the dead king is forbidden to paint a detailed picture of the state in which he suffers. He may go no further—and in this he is quite as effective as any medieval vision of warning—than to hint at "the secrets of my prison house."

Hamlet himself is obsessed by his belief that death inaugurates an existence for the soul which may be even less desirable than life. If death were only sleep, a state of suspension, it would be more desirable than life. No one would choose to endure life,

> But that the dread of something after death—
> The undiscover'd country, from whose bourn
> No traveller returns—puzzles the will,
> And makes us rather bear those ills we have
> Than fly to others that we know not of.[35]

Only at the very end of the play, faced with Laertes' challenge to duel, does Hamlet achieve a sense of resolve which enables him to face death with equanimity: "If it be now, 'tis not to come; if it be not to come, it will be now; if it be not now, yet it will come: the readiness is all."[36]

The picture of an afterlife in which one may suffer greatly is, then, explicit throughout the play; at times it is a paralyzing preoccupation for the prince. At very least, one must conclude that Shakespeare's audience would not have been hostile to the notion of the afterlife, for it is a crucial and indisputable presupposition in the play.

That conclusion seems to be validated if one looks at the burial office of the Elizabethan Book of Common Prayer. The first Book of Edward VI had drastically simplified the Latin offices of the dead in order to excise all traces of the doctrine of purgatory. But a commendation of the "soule to God the father almighty" and of the "body to the grounde" was retained, as was the following versicle and response:

> *Priest.* From the gates of hell
> *Aunswere.* Deliuer theyr soules, o lorde.

The editors of the second Book of 1552 removed these and other suggestions of intercession for the dead in order to be utterly unequivocal in their rejection of purgatory and other notions impinging upon divine choice. The soul is no longer commended to God, although it is still said that "it hathe pleased almightie God of his great mercy to take unto himselfe the soule of our dere brother here departed. . . ." The office remained in this form until 1661.[37] Because of these revisions and residual references to the resurrection and judgment, the office appears to revert to the primitive Christian view of death.

But the case is probably comparable to those of Calvin and, even more nearly, Luther. The doctrine of the soul is not rejected with purgatory and the sacramental system. The object of the revisions was only the notion that the fate of the soul could be influenced by the prayers of the church. Immediate damnation and beatification were, however, not denied, and this idea was probably more prominent in the mind of the sixteenth-century churchgoer than that of the resurrection.

Hamlet's ghost speaks of a purgation of limited duration, a notion which was denied by the official theology of Shakespeare's national church. But the audience understood that doctrine as appropriate to a Catholic king, if only from having heard the polemics of Anglican and Puritan alike against the abuses of Rome. What is more important is that Shakespeare's audience remained close enough to the medieval frame of mind to understand all too well Hamlet's apprehension of being dead: "For in that sleep of death what dreams may come. . . ." They understood as well the significant change represented by the Danish prince's final decision to face death and its consequences: ". . . the readiness is all." One is free to regard fear of the soul's fate as a literary device in *Hamlet*, but he must remember that the images of death and subsequent torment spoke very clearly to the first viewers of the play.

Since the image of death as sleep occurs so prominently in *Hamlet* and, in quite another sense, is roundly attacked by Calvin, it may be well to conclude this historical survey by contrasting the biblical understanding of death as sleep with use of sleep as an image by a theological poet of the generation after Shakespeare.

It will be recalled that "sleep" is a common Old Testament euphemism for death. To sleep with one's fathers or in Abraham's bosom meant to take one's place in the genealogy of Israel and to be remembered according to the evaluation made by history concerning the worth of one's contribution to the life of the People—or, negatively, the nature of one's contribution to Israel's apostasy. In the Old Testament and in the New, death is not regarded as an active state except insofar as one's life influences the continuing life of the People. It was precisely for this reason that "sleep" was a useful figure of speech. In the teaching of Jesus and of Paul, both of whom developed the possibilities for a view of death latent in the traditions of Hebrew apocalyptic, sleep was a figure of the inactive state of the dead before the resurrection when the plan of salvation and restoration was to be fulfilled. In the early church, the figure of sleep retained essentially this significance, although its meaning was complicated by the effort of the Fathers to accommodate the biblical picture of death with the Greek metaphysical doctrine of the soul.

Anyone who has read any of the poetry of John Donne knows of his preoccupation with death. His concern for the subject was not simply metaphorical or metaphysical. Donne posed in a shroud for his effigy, now mounted on the choir-aisle wall of St. Paul's Cathedral, of which he was Dean from 1621 to 1631, in order to dramatize the importance of keeping death foremost in one's mind.

In one of the *Holy Sonnets,* Donne speaks of life as a play, a pilgrimage, and a race which is ended by death's separation of body and soul: "And gluttonous death, will instantly unjoynt/My body, and soule, and I shall sleepe a space." [38] But though "sleepe" may be applicable to the body in Donne's verse, it does not describe the activity of the soule, "my'ever-waking part," which "takes flight" to heaven, leaving "the world, the flesh, the devill."

In another of the sonnets, Donne speaks of "rest and sleepe" as the "pictures" of death. For those who are taken by death, this means: "Rest of their bones, and soules deliverie." [39] But drugs and "charmes" can make man sleep as efficiently as Death's "poyson, warre, and sicknesse." And in any case, the sleep is only temporary, for, as drugs and charms wear off, so Death's sleep and his power will be ended by the eternal awakening. In both sonnets, sleep applies to the state of the body before resurrection, but not to the condition of the soul.

Donne's most startling use of the sleep image occurs in a poem which ostensibly describes the relationship of lovers. The poet in this *Song* addresses his beloved at the moment of their uncoupling:

> Sweetest love, I do not goe,
> For weariness of thee,
> Nor in hope the world can show
> A fitter Love for mee:
> But since that I
> Must dye at last, 'tis best,
> To use my selfe in jest
> Thus by fain'd deaths to dye.[40]

The separation of lovers, the disruption of their physical oneness, is like death: it does not signify fatigue or the end of the relationship but the conjunction and separation of body and soul. The lovers' relationship can also be compared with the daily coming and going of the sun, a rhythm in nature which can be counted on to continue, although man can neither hope that his cycle will not end nor reprieve at judgment his wrong use of time. The beloved sighs as they separate, and Donne returns to the notion that the object of his amorousness is like his soul, sighing and slipping away as the body decays. She complains that she wastes her time with him, and the poet cries out in anguish that in her alone resides the value of his life:

> It cannot bee
> That thou lov'st me as thou say'st,
> If in thine my life thou waste,
> Thou art the best of mee.[41]

In the final stanza, it becomes clear that Donne has not been speaking of the soul as an image for his beloved but the reverse. The judgment may prove the soul right for having felt that she was wasted upon the body, but in the soul the only hope for the body resides. As lovers uncouple and turn aside to sleep, so the body waits in sleep for its life, the soul. In a sense, however, the two keep each other alive; and, therefore, they cannot be regarded as truly separated, although they cannot awaken unless they are rejoined:

> Let not thy divining heart
> Forthinke me any ill,
> Destiny may take thy part,
> And may thy feares fulfill;
> But thinke that wee
> Are but turn'd aside to sleepe;
> They who one another keepe
> Alive, ne'r parted bee.[42]

Over fifteen hundred years lie between the last biblical texts which employ sleep as an image of death and Donne's *Song*. The latter is influenced by many kinds of sources, not the least of which was the use in exegesis and in mystical theology of erotic language to describe the relation of man to God or of man's body to his soul. Nevertheless, Donne's sleep images dramatize the distance between the original approach to death and that of the end of the Reformation era. For at first, the whole man slept; and, if the early Fathers complicated the view of death by introducing the doctrine of the soul, they also insisted on the soul's essential quiescence during its separation from the body. For Donne, only the body truly sleeps; the soul, which is the more important element of human life, is active but also loyal to the body as its lover. The medieval tendency to regard death as the beginning of a period of active, incorporeal existence for the soul and resurrection as the ratification of the soul's judgment had survived the Reformation attack on purgatory and had become the unchallenged Christian mode of explaining the significance of death. Thus, after a long struggle, had Athens overcome Jerusalem.

PART III

The Significance of Death in the Early Christian and Medieval Traditions

1 IMMORTALITY AND RESURRECTION IN THE CHRISTIAN INTELLECTUAL TRADITION

THE PRECEDING ESSAY is an attempt to describe, however inadequately and incompletely, major approaches to the problem of death in the Christian intellectual tradition. The survey has been interrupted rather arbitrarily at about A.D. 1600. It is time to review the results of the historical survey and to suggest some of the problems of interpretation posed by the Christian traditions of speaking of death.

The Christian literature concerning death can only be understood as arising from the confrontation and intermarriage of Hellenism and Hebraism. The concept of immortality is the contribution of the Greek tradition. But even within that tradition two chief kinds of interpretations of immortality must be distinguished. The first, of which Thucydides is typical, regards immortality as the gift of perpetual remembrance by the *polis* to its heroic dead. Plato, who develops metaphysically and metaphorically the doctrine of the mystery religions, represents the other tendency in which the soul is regarded as the immortal and pre-existent element of human nature which resumes its incorporeal existence after its separation from the body and, hopefully, ascends toward truth (or away from corporality) through an educative process.

Both strands of the Greek tradition of immortality were

intimately connected with the social ideals and aspirations of the Greeks. In this respect only can they be said to resemble the Hebraic tradition, which developed no sustained or speculative abstractions within which to describe its understanding of the meaning of death. In the Old Testament writings, the strong sense of the corporate identity of the People dictated that the ancestors of the living be regarded as, in some sense, a part of the continuing, purposeful history of Israel. But beyond this, the Hebrew tradition did not go. The pessimism of the late Wisdom literature and the faith of apocalypticism in a divine act of restoration are best understood as variations upon the main theme to meet the historical exigencies of the political collapse of the elect nation. As for the New Testament evidence, Jesus seems to have developed the apocalyptic view and, at the same time, to have adapted its hope for a divine intervention and restoration. Paul, however, made of the apocalyptic doctrine of the resurrection of the dead a theology of death in which man was regarded as sleeping until the inauguration of the new order. This position, especially as appropriated in the Synoptic Apocalypses, firmly established resurrection as the basic image of the Christian understanding of the meaning of death. However different this point of view may be from the earlier, Hebraic outlook, it remains an insistence on the fact that any afterlife must be conceived in terms of the life of the elect People of God.

From the first, the church Fathers were unable to speak of man other than as a compound of body and soul or of death other than as the separation of these two components. The problem was to treat death and salvation within this framework but without doing violence to the basic picture of death as a sleep before the resurrection. Among the Greek-speaking Christians, Irenaeus accomplished this feat by holding that body and soul await reunion in different places or conditions without imputing an active existence to the soul. Origen, however, in his radically intellectualized approach to the faith rejected the historical and physical as unreal in comparison to the spiritual. Therefore, despite his frequent allusions to the resurrection and Paul's "spiritual body," his system is one in which resurrection is rejected in favor of the doctrine of immortality of the Platonic systems. Origen's view was never accepted precisely because of the radical nature of its accommodation to Hellenistic thought. Thus, at the end of the creative age of Greek patristic thought, Gregory of Nyssa was still struggling to make sense of resurrection and to make room for immortality. More sophisticated than Irenaeus, he nonetheless achieved essentially the same results.

Among the Latin patristic writers, the scriptural emphases were more easily retained because of the Fathers' appropriation of typical Roman attitudes toward morality and history. The judgment of man's historical existence became a primary focus of speculation concerning death and resurrection. At the same time, general insensitivity to the metaphysical problems over which the Greek theologians struggled allowed the Latin writers to speak more freely of the soul's activity during the interim after death. In Tertullian, the feeling for justice is such that the soul must in some sense suffer or be rewarded in the interim before final judgment, but "salvation hinges" upon the flesh, and the full judgment must await resurrection. More moderate and philosophically sophisticated than Tertullian's work, Augustine's teaching stresses the eternal opposition of the two cities and the stabilization of their boundaries by the resurrection. The work of Gregory the Great, heavily influenced by the tradition of contemplation as practiced by the monks, has seemed to some to represent a turning point from primary emphasis on resurrection to stress on the soul's destiny after death. In fact, however, Gregory maintained the general Latin patristic configuration in which the position of the general resurrection was crucial.

Theology in the Early Middle Ages was conservative in method and heroic in attitude. Maintaining the patristic understanding of the soul's destiny after death, the theologians of the period probably also enhanced the importance of the heroic, apocalyptic Last Judgment as the key to understanding death. Thus, in *The Phoenix,* life is understood to be the preparation of a place for oneself in the order which will be inaugurated on Doomsday; and in *Soul and Body,* the soul of the dead man returns to berate the body, which it regards as responsible for the fact that, reunited, they will be found guilty at the judgment. Aelfric of Eynsham, like the author of *Soul and Body,* has the materials from which a picture of incorporeal immortality could be developed; to an extent he does just that, but the eloquence of his treatment of the heroic Doomsday scene is so great as to overshadow and outweigh his description of the disembodied journey of the soul.

It remained for the theologians of the later Middle Ages to shift the center of interest in man's destiny after death from resurrection to the interim before the resurrection, from general to individual judgment. The impetus for this shift was provided by the revival of logical studies and the consequent desire to remove ambiguities and anomalies from the theological tradition and by the emergence of a new piety which emphasized the individual's conscience and found institutional expression in the penitential system and the doctrine of the post-mortem purgation of the soul. In Aquinas's work, therefore, the Doomsday judgment is the ratification and fulfillment of an individual, death-day judgment of the soul which had already instituted a period of suitable reward or punishment of the soul. Dante's *Divine Comedy* articulates the same configuration of events poetically. But the heroic tradition, with subtle changes, remained alive in works such as Langland's *Piers Plowman*.

In the age of the Reformation, it has sometimes been believed that, by attacking the doctrine of purgatory, theologians were returning to the primitive Christian teaching about death. Actually, however, the attack was on the penitential system and the tradition of intercession for the souls of the dead. In the work of Luther and even more clearly in Calvin's *Institutes,* the basic shape of expectations for man after death remained that propounded by scholastic theology in the thirteenth century. Clearly, Shakespeare assumed in writing *Hamlet* that the fate of the soul was, for his audience as for his hero, the primary concern of man in the face of death.

The chief conclusion of this survey is the fact that resurrection remained the chief image for man's destiny after death throughout the first millennium of the Christian era despite the effort to accommodate the doctrine of the immortality of the soul. Only after the revival of logical studies and the emergence of a new, more individualistic piety did the destiny of the soul immediately after death supplant resurrection as the basic element of the understanding of the significance of mortality.

One might suggest that this shift occurred when it did in part because, during the Early Middle Ages, philosophical studies had been in eclipse and men had lost sight of the basic issues between the Hebrews and the Greeks which had constrained early Christians to cling to the image of the resurrection and to subordinate the picture of immortality to the vision of apocalyptic. When the philosophical literature and methodology were revived, men had forgotten what divided Hellenism and Christianity. Recalling only that the Fathers had made a place for immortality as an axiomatic element of the nature of man and desiring to reduce the morass of tradition to a coherent system, the scholastic theologians were unable to see that one of the chief difficulties of the patristic age was the fundamental incompatibility of Greek immortality and Hebrew resurrection. Thus, they were unaware of the significance of their shift of interest from the consummation of history in general to the consummation of the life of the individual.

There has been more than one way of understanding the meaning of death in Christian intellectual history. Or, more accurately, two images for the fate of man after death have competed in the Christian tradition. One might add that immortality and resurrection, the two competing images, were engaged in a protracted struggle for dominance and that the biblical image was not overcome until much later than has often been suggested.

2 THE TRADITION AND PROBLEMS OF INTERPRETATION

I ENDEAVORED IN THE HISTORICAL SURVEY to restrict myself to a phenomenological and descriptive approach. It has not been possible to avoid interpretation, but, on the whole, interpretation has been eschewed in favor of an effort to depict the contours of Christian beliefs about the importance of death as represented in a selection of key documents. There are, however, problems of interpretation—or issues concerning the method of approach and understanding—which must be discussed before the problem of speaking about death and the afterlife in the contemporary world can be attacked or, indeed, before the significance of the early Christian and medieval traditions can be assessed.

Interpretation, in the sense of the extraction of doctrine or moral teaching (which usually implies a judgment of the content thus exposed), has not recently been fashionable in literary and historical circles. Thus, it may be well to explain here what is meant by the term. A historical survey which exposes the existence of competing traditions almost inevitably implies that one or the other is historically more valid or in some other way preferable. Judgments abound as to the relative merits of the images of immortality and resurrection in the Christian intellectual tradition. There have been those who have argued that, because the Bible is unaware of the doctrine of immortality, the adoption of the Greek position by the Christians virtually amounted to apostasy—or at least to a radical adjustment of questionable validity. Another camp has argued (and the argument is as old as Philo) that immortality is implicit in or necessary to Judeo-Christian thought. Still others have urged that the conflict between immortality and resurrection is more apparent than real or that the patristic synthesis adapted immortality in such a way as to appropriate under that canon the basic spirit of the biblical belief in resurrection.[1]

If studies in the history of Christian thought are to be helpful in understanding the developments of the past (I leave aside for the moment the possibility and propriety of their making a contribution to contemporary theological reconstruction), they must attempt to solve these issues. But to do so, the evaluator needs a yardstick, a tool with which he can measure the kinds of changes which have taken place historically and evaluate the importance of those modifications.

In the body of this essay, I propose to search for such a methodological instrument and to approach the problem of interpretation of the kinds of materials which have been set out in the historical essay above. It should be obvious to the reader that both the general understanding of the world—if only because it is pre-Copernican—and the literary approaches of the documents which have been studied are alien to the approaches of our own age. These two observations can serve as starting points. The question may be posed whether the study of world-pictures or of literary forms will yield the kind of evaluatory instrument we need to interpret the meaning and development of Christian attitudes toward death.

METAPHYSICS, COSMOLOGY, AND DEATH: THE PROBLEM OF WORLD-PICTURE

It has already been noted that Plato's doctrine of the soul can only be understood as a part of his metaphysics and epistemology.[2] Plato, in order to posit an absolute truth untouched by the varieties of human opinion,[3] spoke of a realm of Ideas, or Forms, which represented ultimate reality and of which objects and ideas in the world are only reflections. The soul is the rational, nonphysical element or principle in man, which is ungenerate and has fallen from the realm of the Ideas; and the goal of the soul is to remember those truths which it knew originally and, by this process of re-education or recollection, to return to its original state. The doctrine of the soul, to put the matter another way, is the explanation of the manner in which man can hope to contemplate absolute truth. It is, in a sense, the myth which explains how one can have knowledge of reality. In Plato's *Timaeus,* in a rather different mythical framework, the soul's falling away from the realm of the Ideas is used to explain the nature of the created universe, or to draw a cosmological picture.

Together, the doctrine of knowledge and the cosmology of Plato imply a doctrine of salvation in which immortality is a key element. But it is unlikely that the problem of salvation, as later conceived in Hellenism, posed itself as an issue to Plato. His metaphysics and cosmology have religious implications insofar as they posit an ideal manner of life, a discipline through which the soul can realize its potential by return to communication with the Forms from which it has fallen away. Yet Plato's philosophy is not systematic. He has no unified myth or world-picture; and, strictly speaking, his thought is not theistic. It should have been evident in the analysis of the *Phaedo* that, especially when he gives the details of his picture of the soul and its journey, Plato is careful not to commit himself to the myth as a literal picture of the cosmos or of truth.

If it is difficult to pin Plato down on the details and overall structure of his view of the universe, it becomes doubly difficult to understand exactly what he means by the soul. Is it to be regarded literally, to be taken as a part of a working model of the universe, or as a metaphor for the manner in which men acquire knowledge? The question has long been argued and will continue to be argued. It is important here to be aware of the existence of this grave problem in the interpretation of Plato, but it is not necessary to attempt to discover the answer.

What the very question shows us is that the first important formulation of the doctrine of the soul was dependent upon scientific speculation concerning the nature of knowledge, absolute truth, and the structure of the universe. One might ask whether any doctrine of the soul which rises above primitive animism could be stated without similar metaphysical and cosmological implications. If, as I think, the answer to this query is negative, no teaching about the soul can be understood without an interpretation of the scientific world-picture which it presupposes.

The Hebraic heritage within which the primitive Christian conception of the resurrection of the dead was developed was essentially innocent of metaphysical speculation. Insofar as Plato's teaching had theistic implications, it can be said that his God is an abstraction, the principle of cosmic order and truth. Israel, however, conceived of God as a personal being whose primary concern was with historical events in the world. There was no developed cosmological picture, although there were myths in which God was conceived as dwelling among a host of beings who served as his court and although there seem to be relics of an earlier understanding of creation as the imposition of order upon chaos. Man, in the Old Testament view, received his knowledge of Yahweh by revelation and through interpretation of the course of historical events. There was, therefore, no need, epistemologically, to posit a bipartite human nature with a soul to gain knowledge of truth, for truth was known in the historical realm. The goal of existence was also historical, and, for that reason, the notion of an afterlife was not developed and probably inconceivable to most of the Hebrews. Indeed, resurrection, or the revivification of the whole man to participate in a transformed historical existence, is not so much an idea of the afterlife as an extension of the implications of salvation within history. One could develop a metaphysics from this view of existence, but to do so would be to schematize and intellectualize in a manner which is utterly alien to the biblical tradition.

The emergence of the gospel from Palestine coincided with a revival of Plato's thought in the Hellenistic schools and its transformation into a religion by means of systematization and by placing more clearly than Plato had done a supreme being over and above the realm of the Ideas. The Hellenistic Platonists, probably under the influence of the generally pessimistic temper of the times,[4] also tended to go much further than Plato had gone in denigrating the value of the physical world. Man's hope lay in the possibility of the soul's return to its source, the hope for escape from the physical realm. In one way or another, all the thought of the age—from the Gnostics and the mystery cults to the Middle Platonists and Plotinus—was agreed on this point and upon a general cosmic picture or myth which allowed for the possibility of such a return. What may have been metaphoric or exemplary to Plato had become standard doctrine.

Thus, the church Fathers were faced with the necessity of reconciling the irreconcilable. Something has already been said about the manner of their accommodation of the promise of resurrection with the concept of the soul. What remains unexplored and unexplainable is the significance of that accommodation. It was thought by the historians of the eighteenth and nineteenth centuries, whether they sided with Jerusalem or with Athens, that the two were incompatible and that the one compromised the other. The problem is more complex than either Gibbon or Harnack knew, but it remains a problem. Was it possible to explain resurrection in the light of the doctrine of the soul without utterly undermining the Hebraic understanding of salvation in history? Can the result of the confrontation be regarded as recognizably the same gospel?

Gregory of Nyssa felt keenly that this world is both illusory and unreal and regarded the contemplation of ultimate reality as man's proper pursuit.[5] Despite the careful metaphysical sophistication with which he managed to preserve a place for the resurrection of the dead, salvation clearly lies outside the historical realm of space and time and is of a quality essentially discontinuous with the present life. One might even charge Gregory with sophistry in comparison with the radical honesty of Origen. Are we, then, to conclude that, in fact, Nyssa, like Origen, radically transformed or Platonized the Christian understanding of man and the meaning for man of death within the framework of a doctrine of resurrection? How are we to assess his efforts to make room for the resurrection?

Even the crass literalism of the early medieval pictures of the Last Judgment presupposes a residuum of the Greek doctrines that reality is spiritual and that salvation must occur beyond time and space. If the writing of the Early Middle Ages has in common with Jewish apocalyptic a certainty that the whole man must be saved, it has substituted for the Jewish faith in salvation within history the notion that the quality of one's earthly life will determine whether one will successfully transcend the historical order. In this it is indebted through the monks to the Neoplatonic world-picture. But may not the urgency with which it puts the case for righteousness and pictures the retribution with which unrighteousness must be punished bring the theology of this period in effect closer to the Hebraic understanding of the resurrection? And, if so, how is one to assess the effect of the world-picture on the content of theology?

The Christian understanding of death has undoubtedly been radically affected by the world-views of the times in and for which the theologians have spoken. The matter, then, is not simply one of conflict between the basic images of resurrection and immortality. It is far more complex because the metaphysical and cosmological variables not only color the choice of images of a given period but also determine the manner in which the image will be treated.

It remains to be seen whether a more general world-view or basic attitude toward life, and therefore death, can be separated from the metaphysic or world-picture. For the present, the matter may be set aside with the remark that the interpretation of what a given document says about death is made more difficult because analysis of its phenomenology does not necessarily lead us to an accurate understanding of its meaning within the culture for which it was written. Yet there seems to be no clear-cut key to the problem of interpretation and evaluation in the approach by way of the study of world-pictures.

DREAMS AND VISIONS OF THE AFTERLIFE: THE PROBLEM OF LITERARY CRITICISM

One of the possible solutions to the difficulties raised in the preceding section is that theological language ultimately rests upon metaphor and should not be taken as painting a literal picture but as expressing a general set of attitudes. As an approach to this problem, and as a topic which cannot be escaped in any discussion of Christian views of death and the afterlife, the problem of interpretations of dreams and visions which purport to reveal the future of man may fruitfully be discussed. Perhaps a study of the dream as a literary form in the literature about death will open the way to an interpretation of the history of reflections on death.

From the age of the patriarchs to the age of the psychoanalysts, dreams and visions of the afterlife or communications with the dead have often been considered warranties of immortality. Such phenomena apparently occur even among modern secular persons.[6] An assessment of the validity of such phenomena is beyond the scope and intention of this discussion, but it will be possible to say something about the literature of dreams and visions in the period covered in the historical essay of Part II.

The Greek and Hebraic traditions were agreed on the importance of dreams, and the Christians from the first were enabled by this agreement to adapt the Hellenistic dream-lore. It was one area in which Christianity and the culture were not at odds.[7] As early as Tertullian's treatise *On the Soul,* this tendency is evident. Since sleep is a "model" of death, it gives clearer testimony than the philosophy of Plato of the immortality of the soul; for in sleep, "the soul is circumstanced in such a manner as to seem to be elsewhere active, learning to bear future absence by a dissembling of its presence for the moment." [8] In like wise, awakening from sleep presages the resurrection. When the body rests, the soul "disdaining a repose which is not natural to it, never rests," [9] but participates in dreams. True dreams—which are to be tested by their correspondence "to the actual grace of God"—are divinely sent. Most of what is accurate in the pagans' natural theology is, according to Tertullian, derived from the revelation of dreams.[10] Nevertheless, the majority of dreams are false and can be attributed to the work of demonic forces. It is through discipline and sobriety, rather than ecstatic excitement, that one may best prepare himself for fruitful dreaming.

Reference has already been made, although in quite another connection, to two of the most important dream sequences in classical literature: the conclusions of Plato's and Cicero's *Republic.* The latter of these works was lost throughout the Middle Ages except for the *Dream of Scipio,* its final book. The passage claims to be a vision of the ultimate destiny of the soul and to give the sanction for responsible civic conduct. The *Dream of Scipio* was admired on its own merits throughout the medieval period, but its chief influence was exercised through a fourth-century commentary upon it by Macrobius.[11] Macrobius' work, which contains an expert compilation of late classical teaching concerning the significance of dreams,[12] served medieval writers as an authoritative source, and can serve our purposes both as background for the medieval developments and as an introduction to the use of dreams and visions by Gregory the Great.

The body of Macrobius' *Commentary* "is an encyclopedia of general information and an exposition of the basic doctrines of Neoplatonism," [13] but the early chapters of the first book deal with the dream framework of the Ciceronian text. The commentator notes at the outset the similarities between the dreams of Ur in Plato and of Scipio in Cicero and that the former is the report of a man who had apparently died but was restored to life, whereas the latter is a dream. Both devices, Macrobius concedes, are fictional: Plato after depicting the ideal state shows with his "closing fable . . . whither the soul goes on leaving the body . . . in order to show that rewards for the pursuit of justice and penalties for its neglect await the souls of men, for these are indeed immortal and must submit to judgment"; and Cicero discusses the government of the Roman Republic and concludes with a dream which reveals whither "the souls of those who have served the republic prudently, justly, courageously, and temperately . . . must return." [14]

Although critics had ridiculed both authors for their resort to fable or fiction, such devices are not to be scorned if they direct the reader to virtue or treat truth "in a fictitious style." [15] Indeed, it is a philosophical convention "to employ [fabulous] narratives when speaking about the Soul, or about spirits having dominion in the lower and upper air, or about gods in general." [16] That which defies description must be treated in such a manner—although it would be blasphemous to deal in this fashion with "the Supreme God and Mind," [17] the highest being in the Neoplatonic hierarchy.

Five kinds of dreams have been recognized by the tradition: the enigmatic, the prophetic, the oracular, nightmare, and apparition.[18] The latter two are to be dismissed. Nightmares are often induced by overindulgence in food or drink, by erotic fantasy, or by anxiety; and apparitions are phenomena of the "moment between wakefulness and slumber." [19] In an oracle, a holy being reveals what action one should or should not take; a dream is prophetic if it comes true; it is enigmatic if its content requires "an interpretation for its understanding." [20] Further subdivision of enigmatic dreams is possible according to the nature of their applicability. The dream of Scipio fits all the reliable categories. Macrobius concludes with a few observations on the dream as a function of the soul "partially disengaged from bodily functions during sleep." [21] The rest of his work is an exposition of the enigma of Scipio's dream, which is a revelation of the Neoplatonic cosmos.

It should be noted that Macrobius has slipped silently from his initial observation that the dream in Cicero's work is a literary device, a fable which serves to depict the indescribable rewards of the good citizen, to an apparent acceptance of the passage as an actual dream. Herein precisely lies the problem of the interpreter of the literature, theological or imaginative, which purports through dreams to reveal what is in store for man after death. Is he to read the reports of dreams as devices which enable the reporter to describe the indescribable, or is he to consider the dreams as revelations of what is actually in store for man after his death?

With this problem in mind, it is necessary to look once more at the work of Gregory the Great. The treatment of the *Dialogues* above took the form of a summary of its teaching and avoided the "experimental" evidence upon which Gregory based his case.[22] Gregory argues that those who have no first-hand knowledge of spiritual truth must rely upon their elders in the faith and proceeds to base his argument in large measure upon the visions and dreams of reliable contemplatives. Nevertheless, he is not unaware of a tradition of dream interpretation comparable to that upon which the early chapters of

Macrobius' *Commentary* are founded.[23] The chief differences are two. First, Gregory's categories of dreams are divided in accordance with the manner in which they are generated, though Macrobius' classification has more to do with content. Second, Gregory is rather more explicit than Macrobius in his warnings concerning the possibility of being deceived by dreams. Hence, whereas Macrobius tests dreams by their appropriateness to the dreamer, Gregory relies more upon the reputation of the dreamer or visionary for saintliness. It is probably also significant that Gregory first formulated his position on dream-lore in his great work of biblical exegesis, the *Moralia in Job*,[24] and that the passage in *Dialogues* is simply a quotation from the *Moralia*.

Nor is Gregory unaware that the truth displayed by dreams is often metaphorical. He states clearly at one point that the appearance of a ship to a dying man as a vehicle to convey his soul is an expression in physical language of spiritual truth.[25] The journey of the soul is an abstraction which is symbolically represented in dreams by physical pictures. As a sometime biblical exegete, Gregory the Great was well aware that phenomena have various kinds or levels of meaning and that physical pictures often express abstract facts. One must, then, read his work more carefully than those who have attacked his credulity. He is working within classical conventions, and it is not proper to discuss his reports simply "as the silly fables of credulous times." [26]

Gregory tells of a Roman deacon, Paschasius, whose piety was exemplary throughout his life except for one fault: he had supported and remained loyal to the losing candidate in a papal election. When Paschasius died, a miracle of healing occurred at his bier. But much later, a bishop who was at the hot baths met the late deacon and was told that he was suffering for his sin and needed the help of the bishop's prayers. Since Paschasius never again appeared at the baths, the prayers are assumed to have been efficacious.[27] The tale of the visionary appearance of Paschasius allows Gregory to speak of the necessity of expiation for minor sins by men who are otherwise righteous and introduces the subject of the increased clarity of spiritual understanding as the end of history approaches.[28] The details of the story are too well integrated for the reader to ignore the author's literary methods, especially the use of dream-vision conventions.[29]

In the Middle Ages the problems raised by the conventions of the dream framework and the interpretation of dreams are even more complex. For one thing, most of the nontheological literature of the age which deals either directly or indirectly with the problem of death is presented in a dream framework or the framework of a vision or revelation. The apocryphal *Vision of Paul* is such a revelation. This document was recognized by many as heterodox; [30] yet the soul-body *topos* depends upon it, and even Dante either knew it firsthand or relied upon a similar conceptual system. Langland's narrator in *Piers Plowman* is a dreamer whose visions rarely exhaust at one time any single aspect of truth, but cumulatively they do explore the truth about the quest of salvation in its entirety. Geoffrey Chaucer and the poets of medieval romance usually use the dream device and often cite Macrobius as the authority for their poetic practice. But Chaucer, in the *Nun's Priest's Tale,* parodies the conventions of dream interpretation. In the *Summoner's Prologue,* he adapts a fairly common device of making a vision of the afterlife the vehicle for a scatological joke at the expense of the friars. Rabelais was later to parody such visions in his *Pantagruel.* Alongside this rich and varied development of the classical and Christian dream-vision tradition, there stands the scholastic theology which put into a metaphysical and logical context as literal and necessary truth the very kinds of teachings about the soul which the Neoplatonic, contemplative, and literary traditions had spoken of as metaphoric for the inexpressible journey of the soul.

Analysis of the dream conventions and forms is clearly

an important aspect of the effort to understand all this literature. But it raises as many problems for final interpretation as it solves when one attempts to reach some general understanding of the intention of the authors concerned.

It might be possible, drawing upon the world-picture or metaphysics and cosmology of a given period and treating carefully the literary context of dreams and visions, to reach some sort of hypothetical conclusion as to their proper interpretation. Yet it seems to me unlikely that such results would be indisputable or conclusive. A method of this sort would have to rely upon isolation of those elements of, say, a dream vision which are attributable to the world-picture of the age in which it was written. In the case of Gregory the Great, this would mean that one would isolate his version of the Neoplatonic picture of the structure of the cosmos and its spiritual realities.

When the critic has finished, he is left with utterly abstract propositions concerning immortality which make no sense without their cosmological framework. And then he is tempted anachronistically to bring the Freudian system of dream analysis or some other apparatus from our own world-picture to bear upon the problem of analysis and interpretation. The results of such a method of study would be like those of Rudolf Bultmann's biblical studies. When Bultmann had stripped away the mythological framework or world-picture, he beheld a statement of his own brand of twentieth-century existentialism. Something better is required.[31]

CHRISTIANITY AND THE REPRESENTATION OF REALITY: THE FIGURAL APPROACH

There is a third approach from which the kind of critical tool we need can be developed. It is, again, an approach developed in the context of literary criticism. Erich Auerbach,[32] the great German literary critic who was discharged by the Nazis in 1935 and taught thereafter in Turkey and the United States, studied very closely the realism of European literature and the reasons for the unique concern of Western art to interpret the real by means of literary imitation. He believed that the sources of literary realism, or "mimesis," were to be found in circumstances related to the rise and spread of Christianity. I hope in this section to demonstrate that Auerbach's findings can provide us with a useful index for evaluating the basic Christian approaches to the problem of death.

Early Christianity inherited from Judaism its sacred literature, the collection of historical works and works of historical interpretation which we call the Old Testament. That literature both claims for itself a supreme authority and requires interpretation to make clear the significance of its contents for Christians. The biblical books accept what they relate as historical, and the authors place historical events into a universal context between the beginning and the end of creation. The "interpretation" of these historical reports of events within this continuum "becomes a general method of comprehending reality" [33]—a method which serves generally the same purposes, but to an utterly different result, as Greek philosophical reflection. Whereas Greek literature and aesthetic theory tended toward stratification of style based upon the intellectual and social background of the subject portrayed, the effect of the unique Hebraic understanding of the significance of historical event did not encourage such tendencies to formalization and stylistic stratification. The escape of slaves from Egypt was an event of supreme significance; the execution of an insignificant Galilean itinerant rabbi was the occasion of universal salvation. The sublime style of Greek literature simply could not describe such occurrences. Biblical events, without regard to their apparent significance or the grandeur of their setting, have meaning which far transcends what one would expect of the human actors in those events. Within the framework of universal history, they take on new and far more important dimensions. It is in its assertion that mundane events have universal meaning that the unique core of Judeo-Christian thought and religion resides.

Paul, in his confrontation with the Gentiles (or at least with radically Hellenized Jews), met the problem of communicating the meaningfulness of events in the ethnic history of his people to peoples of utterly different origin to whom Hebrew history was of little interest *per se*.[34] In I Corinthians 10:1-11, for example, the apostle speaks of the experience of the Hebrews in the desert of Sinai. He regards these events, including the fact that Moses' followers received "supernatural" food and drink, as unquestionable historical data. But the desert experience of the Jews has as well a larger significance of immediate concern to the Gentile Christians "upon whom the end of the ages is come." It prefigures the nourishment of the new People and their coming into the new land of promise, the Kingdom of God. The events of the Hebrew experience are figures of Christian experience.

> Figural interpretation establishes a connection between two events or persons, the first of which signifies not only itself but also the second, while the second encompasses or fulfills the first. The two poles of the figure are separate in time, but both, being real events or figures, are within time, within the stream of historical life. Only the understanding of the two persons or events is a spiritual act, but this spiritual act deals with concrete events whether past, present, or future, and not with concepts or abstractions; these are quite secondary, since promise and fulfillment are real historical events, which have either happened in the incarnation of the Word, or will happen in the second coming. Of course, purely spiritual elements enter into the conceptions of ultimate fulfillment, since "my kingdom is not of this world"; yet it will be a real kingdom, not an immaterial abstraction; only the *figura,* not the *natura* of this world will pass away. . . , and the flesh will rise again.[35]

The figural interpretation of the Old Testament became the standard method of biblical exegesis in the primitive church. In the Greek world, this approach encountered a superficially analogous Hellenistic tradition of allegorical interpretation, and the two competed in an extremely subtle manner throughout the Middle Ages. In the allegorical approach, it does not matter whether the event interpreted is historical; indeed, most medieval allegories personify abstractions such as moral virtues or vices. In the Greek schools, myths had long been interpreted allegorically as objectifications of spiritual truth, and Philo had Hellenized Judaism by finding an allegorical presentation of Platonism in the Torah. The Alexandrian exegetical school, of which Origen was the chief exemplar, tended to divest events "of their concrete reality" and to replace "the law and history of Israel . . . by a mystical or ethical system." [36] Whereas figuralism saw one event as fulfilling another, allegorism saw event as a veil concealing abstract truth. For example, the Passover events were to the figuralists a foretokening of the work of Christ and of man's salvation; but to the allegorizer, they veiled or symbolized the journey of the soul. The reality of the historical event, which is at the core of figuralism, is of no concern in allegory, which is often even embarrassed by physical existence and, at least in the Hellenistic schools, attempts to get around its embarrassment by negating the significance of phenomena.

Auerbach argued that the figural method endowed the history of the Hebrews with significance for peoples remote from ancient Israel in time and place. Figurally interpreted, events from creation to the birth of Christ were essential to the understanding of the present history of all Christians. So it is (to take an example Auerbach does not cite) that the Germanic historian Gregory of Tours prefaced his *History of the Franks* with an account of Hebrew and ecclesiastical history in order to set the history of his people in the only context in which it assumed meaning. The device was hardly unusual; it was necessary to the historian's understanding of the importance of his own age. A clue to his interpretation of his national history is provided by his description of the baptism of the Merovingian ruler, Clovis, who goes to the baptismal font a "new Constantine . . . , to blot out the former leprosy, to wash away in this new stream the foul stains borne from old days." [37]

As this reference to Constantine as the figure of Clovis indicates, the figural interpretation of events came to be applied to postbiblical occurrences. All events are to be interpreted in the light of the universal history of salvation. A happening such as the conversion of Constantine is a figure of the conversion of another Gentile ruler; and, because both events are "provisional and incomplete," it also points to "a promise of the end of time and the true kingdom of God." [38]

Figuralism endows historical event with meaning. Although in a sense it might be regarded as undermining interest in historical process for its own sake by insisting on universal and ultimate ends, nevertheless it gave Christians the rationale for their belief in the urgency of event and action and constantly recalled their attention from the eternal to the mundane. It provided a device which enabled them to resist the prevailing view that life in the flesh is of little real importance. So it is that in Christian literature one finds again and again capsule universal histories of the chief events and personages from Adam to Doomsday which help to explain present history. And so, too, it is that, as in the medieval mystery plays, homey touches of realism (Noah's squabbling with his wife and her reluctance to board the ark, the poverty and daily concerns of the shepherds who go to the Bethlehem manger) become inseparable elements of the depiction of events in the history of salvation which are also figures of our salvation. The implication is "that every occurrence, in all its everyday reality, is simultaneously a part in a world-historical context through which each part is related to every other, and thus is likewise to be regarded as being of all times or above all time." [39]

Thus, the classical tradition of the high, or sublime, style of serious subject matter and the low, or humble, style of comedy could not be maintained in the tradition of Christian letters. Perhaps the tensions are best seen at work in the medieval religious drama. The mystery plays which generally depict biblical events are inevitably figural in their tendency to emphasize the ordinary characteristics of the events depicted and to underscore their relevance to present history. The allegorical impetus to generalization and schematization was, however, at work when the genre of the morality play developed. These plays depict the struggle of a representative man to withstand the onslaughts of the vices and to gain salvation. In the *Everyman,* the best and purest example of the form in English, there are realistic notes, but the abstractness of the personifications is unusually complete. But the morality play was also influenced by the figural propensities of the Christian imagination, and the characters representing the vices often became completely realistic. It is in such characters that historians have found the precursors of Falstaff, the greatest English comic character. The example of the drama has its analogues in all the literary types.

The seriousness with which the Christian imagination took the events of the past—the sacred history and secular events of great importance—influenced the consideration of present events and of the general situation of mankind. The life of man in history was imbued with importance and urgency because it had a place in the larger plan of history, a place in the continuum between the beginning and the end. Whether explicitly or implicitly, that importance and urgency were underlined by a tendency to deal directly with the mundane and the specific.

Strictly defined, the figural *method* requires an explicit relationship between two historical events. As a matter of fact, one can distinguish what might be called a figural *attitude* in which present historical events and the general condition of mankind are implicitly caught up into the significance of the universal history of salvation. The mystery plays, for example, employ the figural method, but the moralities betray the figural attitude. In this attitude, I suggest, lies the key to examining and testing Christian documents to determine whether or not they maintain what is at the core of the Judeo-Christian view. Does a given writing provide an interpretation of day-to-day events within a universal, historical framework?

It can be argued that this method is impressionistic and that it will rely upon a potentially subjective evaluation of the tone of a given document. The allegation must be granted a limited validity. At the same time, however, it must be argued in reply that the use of the figural attitude as a means of interpreting the Christian approaches to death will provide an index independent of the complexities of world-picture and the details of literary form. It is based upon an attitude toward historical event and implies a fairly strict method of interpreting historical events.

If one reviews quickly the documents which were examined in Part II, it becomes clear that the retention of the primitive Christian image of resurrection of the dead does not necessarily result in maintenance of the sense of historical purposiveness which lay behind the biblical belief in resurrection and which presupposed the figural attitude.

The Greek Fathers, for all their care to safeguard resurrection as the key to understanding the meaning of death, were deeply influenced by the embarrassment of the later Platonists with the historical and the physical. To be sure, they recognized the dangers implicit in the Platonic approach and would not tolerate extreme forms of Docetism and Gnosticism; but, at the same time, they tended toward an accommodation of Hellenistic idealism and spiritualism which, in effect, undermined the importance of the historicity of their Judaic heritage. As one might expect, the tendency is not so pronounced in the earlier Fathers like Irenaeus, who clearly argues from within the figural framework. But even Irenaeus sees the true purpose of Christ's work as the gift of immortality, which makes man fundamentally different from what he is by nature and capable of escaping from the historical to the spiritual.[40] The case is far clearer with Origen, for whom salvation consists of "lifting man up beyond human nature and making him change to a superior and more divine nature,"[41] which is superior precisely because it is not historical but spiritual. For Origen, event can be an allegory of ultimate truth in basest form, but earthly occurrences can never contain in themselves more than the germ and sign of the real, spiritual existence. Similarly, Gregory of Nyssa's effort to reconstruct the doctrine of resurrection to correct Origen's excesses redresses the balance only by returning to something more like the contours of the earlier teaching of resurrection. Beneath that surface, however, there remains a strong feeling that the reality and significance of historical life and events are of minimal consequence compared with the ultimate reality of the spiritual. The historical events which the New Testament writers interpreted figurally tend to be allegorized by the Greek Fathers. They have little or no significance other than as symbols of abstract truths concerning the soul and its quest for salvation. The event pales before its meaning, and its historical significance and urgency tend to slip away. For all their efforts to retain the outline of the resurrection, the early Greek theologians shared the Platonists' distrust of the historical as against what they regarded as ultimate reality. What finally concerned them was the soul's release and escape from flesh and history into a far more significant mode of being.

The Latin Fathers in some ways gave more ground than the Greeks to the image of the immortal soul and yet were more seriously concerned with the problem of moral performance within history. Therefore, they were able to maintain the figural attitude more clearly than their Greek-speaking colleagues. Tertullian grants the immortality of the soul and its capacity for a separate, disembodied existence. But resurrection is the central image for him because "life is the cause of judgment" [42] and the same man who participated in life must face the consequences of his historical action. Augustine's position is far more complex because of his grappling with the problems of time and the will. Nevertheless, one's allegiance in history to one or another of the two cities prefigures his eternal lot. Gregory the Great had a vivid sense of the urgency of his troubled times which forced him to abandon his contemplative desire for withdrawal from the world in order to seek spiritual perfection.[43] Despite his oft-repeated belief that the soul's nurture and destiny is man's highest concern, one feels that he really believed that man's duty in the world of events has priority and fixes one's destiny. In other words, the Latin theologians seem not to have struggled so hard to maintain the contours of New Testament theology as did the Greeks, but (almost despite themselves) they accorded a far greater importance to the events of life in the world.

The literature of the early medieval church has at its very core the figural method and the consequent belief in the significance of historical performance within the scheme of salvation. *The Phoenix* is a figural interpretation of a phenomenon which its author regarded as historical and as betokening the importance of life for setting one's ultimate destiny. So, too, the *Soul and Body* poem, with its emphasis on the details of physical corruption and the consequences of sinfulness, thinks of death not as the opening of new doors to the soul but as fixing the destiny of the whole man, whose future is determined by his performance in history. Aelfric of Eynsham, who had the materials to elaborate a consistent picture of the post-mortem adventures of the soul, seems similarly to have been more concerned to stress the heroic picture of judgment as the fulfillment of life.

In the High Middle Ages, the pattern in which expectations concerning death were presented changed. The picture of the soul's destiny after death supplanted the picture of resurrection as the chief image. In Thomas Aquinas it is difficult to say exactly what this shift means for what we are calling the figural attitude or the feeling that historical events have a significance within the universal and historical scheme of salvation. Probably, however, the fact that Thomas's picture of the soul's destiny is so closely connected with the doctrine of purgatory and the sacramental system of penance indicates that Thomas's substitution of immortality for resurrection did not have the same kinds of consequences which had threatened Greek theology. If it is legitimate to compare Thomas's position with Dante's, this suggestion is validated. For Dante's vision of the scholastic afterlife is, as Auerbach has shown, profoundly and essentially figural. The *Piers Plowman* of Langland, which maintains a rather old-fashioned theological framework and yet is a product of the new piety, is as explicitly figural as the *Comedy*. Man in the world, for Langland, stands poised between ultimate reward and punishment, constantly aware of his relationship with the events of sacred and profane history. Despite the shift of images from resurrection to immortality, then, the medieval writers on the whole maintained the figural attitude.

The case is not so clear in the sixteenth century. I think it can safely be said that Luther retained the medieval figural attitude. Yet Calvin, despite his formal affinities to medieval theology and the high seriousness with which he and his followers undertook to realize their vision of a purified, historical church and society, seems to have lost the figural sense of the importance and value of the everyday. Perhaps the removal of teaching about the sacraments from its medieval place as part of the doctrine of salvation to the section on ecclesiastical polity is symbolic of the undermining of the figural feeling for the contextual interrelatedness of phenomena by the elevation of the notion of eternal, divine election. Somehow the individual stands alone awaiting the revelation at death of a doom already decreed. In Shakespeare's *Hamlet,* the tragic and problematic view of life clearly supplants the figural. The dénouement of history in the figural view was the resolution of issues raised by historical existence.[44] But Hamlet's problems arise from within himself and are tragically resolved by the interaction of his character and his situation. He and his world are self-contained; and he is not understood in the light of other events or figures, nor is his destiny to be resolved by the judgment which is the fulfillment of the meaning of all events. His apprehensiveness about what will happen after death seems to be unrelated to the figures by which such apprehensions had formerly been interpreted.

In the early Greek church and in the age of the Renaissance, then, the fundamental Judeo-Christian understanding of the importance of mundane events within the scheme of salvation tended to be undermined. In both cases, the image chiefly employed to explain the meaning of man's death was the immortality of the soul, but the reasons for the loss of the feeling of the urgency of one's life and actions were rather different in these two cases. For the former the cause lay in the Hellenistic mistrust of the historical and physical and the belief that reality lay completely outside history. The physical world could only symbolize the real world of spiritual truth. The Renaissance did not deny the reality or the importance of historical event, but it lost the feeling that events are interrelated and derive their meaning from their place within universal history. Both the event and the individual seem to be autonomous or self-contained, subjects for examination in isolation, rather than within a figural relationship to other events.

3 LIFE AND DEATH IN CHRISTIAN THOUGHT

IF IT IS TRUE that the figural attitude provides a clue to the interpretation or evaluation of Christian reflections on death, it might be remarked by way of conclusion that, like the Old Testament, the Christian tradition is really quite unconcerned with death as a subject for reflection. The best Christian teaching about death has always been teaching about life. Life in the world is ultimately the most important part of man's existence. It assumes a frightening urgency and importance because the life of every man is a part of and contributes to the great historical drama of salvation. If Christians pointed to the bodies on which worms fed in the grave and spoke endlessly about the transitoriness of life and the pleasures of the world, it was only to point out how important it was to live well now: there is only one chance.

It cannot be denied that Christian teachers have worked out a theology of rewards and punishments which has colored their teachings. The recompense for right living in history is the goal of history, the kingdom of God, or the eternal well-being of the soul. On the whole, however, Christian theology is goal-oriented and not process-oriented or task-oriented. It looks to a transformed historical order and stresses the vital importance of acting in history so as to become a figure of the goal. When Christian thought has been preoccupied with the tasks and processes of achieving salvation, it has lost hold of the sense of historical urgency and, I would argue, of the genius of its heritage.

To make this judgment is to seem to be hard on the mystical tradition in Christian thought. Yet, in the West, Christianized Neoplatonism, the frame of reference for the earliest contemplatives and of a number of the Fathers, constantly broke away from its longed-for contemplation of the process of salvation and the task of educating the soul because it could not escape the urgent demands of the drama of history and its goal. One need only remember that two of the greatest Western contemplatives were two of the most important figures in the shaping of medieval society: Gregory the Great and Bernard of Clairvaux. This-worldly concerns often made demands which were unavoidable even by those who had given themselves over to other-worldly pursuits.

The meaning of death is to be found in life. It is what one does now that sets his judgment and gives him a place in a history which runs from the beginning of time to its end. Death, then, is a threat to the living only because it is the end of life, which is fraught with importance not alone for the living individual but also for the entire species of which he is a member. To contemplate the fact of death is to understand the importance of living.

PART IV

Toward a Twentieth-Century Acceptance of Mortality

1 DEATH IN THE MODERN PERIOD

IT IS TIME TO ADDRESS OURSELVES once more to the problem of death in the contemporary world.

It will be helpful to bear in mind several observations which have emerged in the course of Parts II and III. First, despite the still-prevalent opinion that Christianity is irrevocably committed to the doctrine of immortality, it has never had a clear-cut or universal commitment. The basic category under which primitive Christians developed a view about the meaning of death was resurrection. That image, which was basically incompatible with the Platonic notion of immortality, competed for over a millennium with the image of immortality; and a theological *modus vivendi* was worked out in which, although the immortality of the soul was adopted as an axiom, the real locus of hope for mortal man was the resurrection of the body. It is true that the doctrine of resurrection lost its hold at the end of the Middle Ages and was almost forgotten until the present century. But this does not necessarily mean that contemporary theology is bound by the consensus of the modern period. There was an ancient and long-sustained tension in Christian thought as to the proper image under which to explore the significance of death, and the fact of that struggle opens options for theological reconstruction.

Second, the tone of Christian reflection on death throughout the Middle Ages characteristically stressed the urgency of one's life in the world as a vital link in the universal history, which stretches from the creation to the inauguration of the Kingdom of God. It is difficult to state the implications of this fact so that the possibility of dangerous misapprehensions can be avoided. It is not so much that one is to live well in order to earn a reward or that he is to be good in order to avoid punishment. The afterlife, whether conceived as immortality or as resurrection, has always been a sanction for living well in the present. But in the best of Christian theology and poetry, the accent has not been on hedging one's bets or seeking out the safe way. Rather a sense of urgency has been associated with life in the world in the light of the Creator's intentions for his creation—an urgency which requires of men a creative boldness, a willingness to take risks. The stakes are great not because of what will happen to the individual, but because what the individual does is important in the whole history of mankind. It was the achievement of the figural point of view that it linked the most common elements of the life of the most common man intimately and directly to the great moments of the sacred history and made clear the vital importance of living and dying well and boldly.

Third, it is clear from our perspective that Christian thought has been able to adapt its imagery for speaking of death to the world-pictures of the several chief periods of its history. The surface pattern of Christian reflection on death has depended on the metaphysics and the cultural conditions of the age. What seems, then, to be more important than the differences in images for death is the maintenance of the élan or tone by which life has been given its urgency and within which the meaning of death has been shaped. I would argue, in other words, for a kind of theological relativism which is more concerned to continue the *tone* of traditional teaching about death than either its outward form or its content because both of these latter conditions are dictated not by the terms of eternal truth but by temporal or social and cultural and even economic determinants.

MODERN MAN AS THE LONELY PERCEIVER

These are generalizations which seem to be validated by the historical study of the attitudes of Christians toward death. Now, before proceeding to suggestions for the formulation of a present attitude, it is necessary to attempt to characterize the world-picture of the modern period.

The point at which the historical sampling or survey of Part II of this volume was interrupted was the eve of a sweeping change of basic attitudes and patterns of thought. Hitherto, intellectual argument had been based on authority of two kinds: the authority of the Christian tradition or revelation and the authority of the logical method. The change, which began with the work of Descartes and was more clearly manifested by the thought of Newton, Locke, Berkeley, and Hume, might be comprehended under the general rubric of empiricism. The authority for intellectual arguments and programs of action was no longer external; experience and observation were the new sources and validators of authority. What one knew to be true was that which he had seen and experienced. Thus, a new science, a new politics, a new economics and commerce, a concept of toleration—new modes of thought and existence—came into being.

One of the effects of this transition was to turn man in upon himself. He could know and believe only that which authenticated itself to him by experience. Bishop Berkeley's question, whether a tree falling in a forest made a noise if there was no one present to hear the crashing, could not have made sense two centuries before. In George Berkeley's time, however, it is inconceivable that the question would not have been posed. If there is no hearer is there sound? If the occurrence of the phenomenon is not validated by someone's experience can it be said to have happened? Is not the existence of a thing dependent upon its being perceived? Berkeley got around his problem by working a variation on Platonism or Idealism in which God is Mind, the eternal Perceiver upon whose existence and perception all being depends. The important thing for our purposes is to note that Berkeley's empirical question states the characteristic assumption of modern empiricism: one cannot know anything that is not validated by immediate and personal experience. Depending on the degree of one's skepticism and his estimate of the possibility of communication, the individual is more or less isolated from all other beings. Modern man tends to be the lone perceiver—and not infrequently has he doubted even the correctness of his perception.

This radical individualism and experientialism is more compatible, as one reflects upon the problem of death, with the mode of immortality than with the mode of resurrection. Resurrection is not simply an outrage in the face of reason and experience; it also does not do justice to modern man's sense of aloneness and his general belief that mind or perception is somehow at the core of being.

Characteristically, then, modern theology has spoken of man's immortality rather than his resurrection. Usually, it has been believed that, in so doing, the theologians have continued the teaching of the Reformation or, in the case of Roman Catholicism, the Middle Ages. One of the few eighteenth-century theological writers who tried to reassert the doctrine of resurrection, ironically, illustrates this point. Archdeacon Francis Blackburne, in *A Short Historical View of the Controversy concerning an Intermediate State and the Separate Existence of the Soul between Death and the General Resurrection* (1765) and in other works, argued vigorously and with remarkable clarity for the biblical view of the meaning of death. Blackburne understood that the emphases of his contemporaries, from Catholic to Deist, on immortality were far removed from the biblical position. Yet, in his insistence on the "sleep of the soul" and on the resurrection as "the scriptural system of immortality," Blackburne argued not so much against immortality as a doctrine as against the notion that the soul is active after death. Like many other modern scriptural literalists, the Archdeacon did not attack the individualism of his contemporaries or the idea of immortality as a rational doctrine of natural theology. He simply urged that immortality was not biblical and that true believers, failing to be rigorously scriptural in their theology, had missed an important polemical opportunity. His attack on immortality, in other words, was by no means designed to restore to theology the spirit of early Christian theology (what I have called the figural attitude) but to score a polemical point by observing a nicety of theological topography.

In general, immortality was accepted without question in the modern period. At the one extreme it was supported by the Thomistic realists and at the other by the liberal Protestant idealists. In the latter tradition, the doctrine was sometimes pushed to metaphorical extremes. So, for example, Ludwig Feuerbach, in *The Essence of Christianity* (1841; as translated by the English novelist George Eliot), declared that "Faith in the future life . . . is faith in the freedom of subjectivity from the limits of Nature; it is faith in the eternity and infinitude of personality . . .: consequently, it is the faith of man in himself." Not uncommonly, it was asserted that the very belief in God stood or fell with belief in man's immortality. In the light of the isolation of modern, empirical man, it is not difficult to appreciate the importance he attached to his immortality, for without it he had no God and no escape from self. Only in the "freedom of subjectivity" from natural mortality could man have any self-confidence.

It was not until the first part of the present century that the shape of biblical eschatology was rediscovered by Albert

Schweitzer and others. Much of theological history since then can be understood as an effort to assimilate the biblical picture of death and resurrection into the modern point of view. Given the predispositions of modern empiricism, that is a difficult task; and the general failure of the theologians is to be perceived in the obscurantism and evasiveness of much modern theological talk about death and in the failure of Christians generally to have absorbed what has been said.

DEATH IN THE MODERN NOVEL

Many of the novelists of the late modern period, on the other hand, treated the subject of death without the encumbrance of the theologians' professional stake in or commitment to a metaphysical point of view. It may, then, be useful to look briefly at three modern novels which deal with death and which exhibit quite different attitudes. It is conceivable that they may point the way to a solution of the problem of speaking forthrightly about death in a theological context. These novelists were, as Auerbach argued in *Mimesis,* the inheritors of the figural attitude who broke away from the efforts of seventeenth- and eighteenth-century classicists to divest literature of realism by means of a formalism of style. Thus, in their works, rather than in theology and philosophy, one finds true concern for the everyday life of man.

THOMAS MANN: DEATH IN VENICE

Thomas Mann's *Death in Venice,* written in 1911, is a richly textured and complex novella about the death of Gustave von Aschenbach, a German novelist and intellectual. Despite the care Mann lavished on realistic, descriptive detail and upon ironic contrast between the real and the ideal, his primary concern in the work is with the realm of the unseen, with the experiences of Aschenbach, the inner man. To expose the inner workings of his subject, Mann narrates the work from the carefully restricted point of view of Aschenbach, who conceals from the world both his passion and his fatigue behind a mask of aristocratic serenity and self-assuredness and who is an observer of the world rather than a participant in its activities.

Aschenbach, in the course of an evening stroll, observes at the portal of a mortuary chapel, surrounded by images of death and burial, a man about whose appearance there was "something not quite usual." The stranger's "pilgrim air" inspires in the great writer "a longing to travel" in exotic lands. Casting aside his carefully disciplined life, he journeys first to an island in the Adriatic which does not fulfill his expectations and, thence, to Venice, "the incomparable, the fabulous, the like-nothing-else-in-the-world. . . ." There he encounters a Polish boy whose family is staying at the same hotel on the Lido. Enchanted by "the lad's perfect beauty" which "recalled the noblest moment in Greek sculpture," Aschenbach settles in—after one ill-fated effort to escape—to a routine devoted to observing the lad on the beach, at the hotel, and in the city. An epidemic of cholera grips the city, but Aschenbach's fascination with the boy Tadzio is such that he is unable to leave and, indeed, risks making a fool of himself by his ever-bolder pursuit of the object of his obsession. Finally, as he sits one day on the beach watching Tadzio, who has waded out to the tidal sand-bar, Aschenbach dies just as the boy half turns so that their eyes meet: "It seemed to him the pale and lovely Summoner out there smiled at him and beckoned; as though, with the hand he lifted from his hip, he pointed outward as he hovered on before into an immensity of richest expectation."

No outline can capture the richness of Mann's novella; and the one I have given does not do justice to its mythic overtones, to the complex succession of symbolic personages, or to its pervasive irony. For our rather limited present purposes, we must be content to say something about Aschenbach's sojourn in Venice—his "interim existence" and "means of passing time"—as an adventure of the soul through which is developed a very special point of view as to the meaning of death.

Aschenbach sees a connection between his relationship with Tadzio and the teaching of Socrates in Plato's *Phaedrus* concerning love. For the old man, the boy is the personification and embodiment of beauty. According to Plato, "sight is the keenest mode of perception" (*Phaedrus,* 250d); and, perceiving beauty, we can see a mirror image of reality, of ideal form. The beauty of a Tadzio serves as a reminder of truth and "sets us afire with pain and longing." Aschenbach's opinion on some great aesthetic issue is required by the world for which he writes; and, sitting at a table before his beach house, he writes his opinion by copying in words the "model" of Tadzio: "Strangely fruitful intercourse this, between one body and another mind."

In the *Phaedrus,* Socrates discussed issues concerning love, beauty, immortality, and literary creation. The questions are all raised by a hypothetical issue about the proper love relationship between men, and Socrates asserts that true *eros* is that which turns the soul toward truth and does not succumb simply to physical attractiveness. It must partake of that philosophical discipline which turns the soul from the physical image to the ideal form and enables the souls of both lovers to recollect and to return to the realm of the ideas.

Aschenbach finds in Tadzio that object of *eros* for which his soul has been yearning, and he senses the liberating possibilities of contemplation of beauty through the boy. But, ironically, he is unable to free himself from his passion for the outward form of beauty in order to fulfill his longing. He both overlooks Tadzio's real nature—his sickliness, his bad teeth, his vanity—and surrenders himself to an almost Dionysian pursuit of the sensual in his intoxication with the ideal. He cannot initiate a direct and personal relationship with the boy; and so he follows him at a distance, hovering outside his door at night. He allows his barber to blacken his hair and rouge his cheeks and thus becomes as pathetically ridiculous as the symbolic old man trying to imitate the form of youth whom he had encountered enroute to Venice. A dream reveals to him "in his very soul . . . the bestial degradation of his fall."

Finally, Aschenbach hears again the Socrates of the *Phaedrus* warning that "detachment . . . and preoccupation with form lead to intoxication and desire. . . ." He is somehow changed in that last moment in which he sees Tadzio beckoning him "into an immensity of richest expectation."

Despite the care lavished by Mann on concrete descriptive detail in *Death in Venice,* the novella is an adventure of the soul; and Aschenbach, although affected by what goes on about him, is isolated and absorbed by the problematic nature of his own existence. There is an allusion at the outset to the troubled condition of Europe and to the "tasks imposed upon [Aschenbach] by his own ego and the European soul." But the great writer leaves his setting and his tasks for his "interim existence" under the influence of a death figure. The mystique of Venice, at once enchanted and decadent, is not so much a historical setting as the never-never land of the protagonist's spiritual adventure. The cholera epidemic concerns—even obsesses—him, but he does not act in response to the deathly plague about him except to sink further into his degradation of soul. He baits "the outer world"; and on the morning of his death, he has "a sense of futility and hopelessness—but whether this referred to himself or to the outer world he could not tell." The reality with which Aschenbach must cope is not the reality of events and history but that of idea and spirituality.

The Platonic allusions in *Death in Venice* are, then, not superficial or decorative. The mode of immortality is the author's primary frame of reference. The novella is psychologically realistic; indeed, it is a profound study of the personality of an aging man whose life has been devoted to intellectual pursuits and a devastating commentary on aestheticism. The work is also realistic in its depiction of the physical world. But its subject is the soul of Aschenbach, his struggle to love truth as objectified by Tadzio. The very construction of the work is such that it is virtually impossible to evaluate Gustave von Aschenbach as a man in history, a man whose life and death have some sort of importance in a continuum of meaningful events in the world. His destiny is a spiritual one. What matters is that "immensity of richest expectations" which the soul of Aschenbach has encountered and will eternally encounter.

It does not matter whether Mann believes literally in the immortality of the soul, that the soul of Gustave von Aschenbach will go on forever struggling to attain to the realm of the Ideas. Probably he does not, although there is a sense in which Aschenbach can be regarded as a soul separated from the body after the opening scene when he goes from the cemetery in the city where he lives to an unreal place, moved by the "pilgrim" figure of death. He has been in Venice before, but never before has he approached the city from the sea; thus, his experience there at least partially involves recollection. The important fact for the present discussion, however, is that *Death in Venice* is a picture of life and death which stresses the isolation of modern man and employs the mode of immortality to depict that isolation as a spiritual, nonhistorical struggle for salvation by means of discovery of the ideal form of truth and beauty.

Mann's concern for the spiritual struggle of man is such as to undercut his remarkable realism. Events and objects external to Aschenbach do arouse reaction on his part, but on the whole what is external to the protagonist is either symbolic of what is going on in his consciousness or of the ideal for which he yearns and which beckons to him. Thus, for all its realism—and anyone who has been in Venice knows how miraculously the being of that city is evoked—Mann's depiction of the world points beyond the present and physical to the eternal, and mundane events are without significance of their own in the historical continuum.

LEO TOLSTOY: THE DEATH OF IVAN ILYICH

"The history of Ivan Ilyich's life was most simple, and most common, and most terrible." This disarming sentence, which begins the second section of Leo Tolstoy's *The Death of Ivan Ilyich* (1886), invariably arrests the reader's attention and yet cannot prepare him adequately for the revelation of banality and terror which is to follow. Neither is he prepared for the impact of Ivan's redemption through suffering by the earlier comment that the facial expression of the dead Ivan in his coffin was "a rebuke or reminder to the living."

The Death of Ivan Ilyich begins with the death of its hero. Tolstoy probes first the reactions of Ivan's colleagues and his wife to his death. Ivan Ilyich's death creates a vacancy in the law courts; it is an unwelcome reminder to others of their own mortality; it disrupts the routine of one's social life; it creates a financial burden for his heirs. Only the peasant servant, Gerasim, is willing or able to reflect openly upon the universality of death.

Tolstoy proceeds to show that the life of his hero was as conventional and as superficial as that of his associates. Ivan Ilyich was a man who did all the right things and who used the comforts and social mores of his world to protect himself from conflict. Ivan Ilyich's career, family, and social life were carefully adjusted and manipulated so that he was safe from the unpleasantness of his wife, disappointment with his career, and confrontation with himself. In order "to lead a decent life approved by society, it was necessary to work out a definite attitude."

But, while helping a decorator arrange the draperies in his drawing room so that all would be *comme il faut,* Ivan fell from a ladder and bruised his side. The wound, ignored at first, evidently initiated the undiagnosable illness which, slowly and painfully, led to his death. In the helplessness of his sickness, Ivan Ilyich discovers that he is not the only one who has worked out an attitude. His doctors and his wife—indeed, everyone but Gerasim, who knows that "We're all going to die"—have built up unassailable fortresses of self-defense. The dying man's alienation is complete. Having no other resource, he is now forced to face himself and to re-evaluate his life.

Death in those last days became the only reality, but it had the effect of forcing Ivan Ilyich to examine his life. There were some pleasurable moments of childhood and youth to be remembered, but the comfortable and self-protective years of adulthood seemed "ugly and senseless." His "life kept getting worse and worse. . . . Inversely proportional to the square of the distance from death." Life seemed utterly worthless. After confession and communion, he still felt the hypocrisy of everything in his own life and the lives of those about him.

Three days of horrible screaming followed; the screams proclaimed Ivan's resistance to death. Finally, he admits to the worthlessness and meaninglessness of his life, and there is peace: "What happened to him was what used to happen in a railroad car when he thought he was riding forward but was actually riding backward, and suddenly discovered the real direction." Ivan admits to the wrongness of his life and learns that there is another and better kind of life. That is his saving knowledge. In his last moments, feeling "that it was possible to rectify all this," he recognizes the need to act and—the only possible act left to him—to spare his family further suffering in his behalf. Fear of death disappears—"Instead of death there was light"—and joy takes its place.

This has seemed a curious salvation to some readers. There is no hint of an afterlife of resurrection or immortality in *The Death of Ivan Ilyich*. Life is existence in this world. Thus, the redeemed life of Ivan Ilyich lasts only a few moments and consists of a realization and an action. It is clear, however, that we are intended to believe that it suffices. This is the secret at which the expression on the decaying corpse hints. In that it gives Ivan peace or "light" at the end, it is enough; and in that his state can never change, it is eternal. It does not even matter that no one else knows.

Reality for Tolstoy, unlike Mann, consists of what one sees and knows and is. The conventionality and triviality of Ivan's life are both determined and defined by the objects and the persons about him. He lives—and almost dies—for the intricate but vulgar tapestry of associations and manipulations which he, like everyone else, has woven about himself like a cocoon. The values are clearly wrong, but truth is not something which exists outside the world of Ivan Ilyich or is mirrored for him by personages and objects. A correct ordering of values depends not upon the perception of an ultimate or ideal outside Ivan. It depends upon honesty, and that honesty is something only the protagonist can supply himself by letting down the elaborate defense works which are the entire content of his life.

Ivan Ilyich is, however, like Gustave von Aschenbach in his isolation or alienation. That is only to say that they are both men of the modern age, one seen realistically and the other idealistically (in the technical senses of realism and idealism). Everything is seen and known from the inside out and not, as in earlier centuries when authority and truth were external to the individual, from above and beyond. Even if his society were so inclined, no one had the authority requisite to convince Ivan Ilyich (as, say, Everyman was convinced in the morality play) that his life was vapid and vain. There was no saving him from himself except through the experience of suffering, through which he came to realize in his very loneliness the deceptiveness of his mode of life.

Nevertheless, *The Death of Ivan Ilyich* is more than a psychological study of one man's salvation. It is also a devastating criticism of a conformist society which encourages its Ivans to hide from themselves. The fault of the society is that it accepts notions of propriety and taste as authoritative and exerts pressures which make it difficult to escape from the external authorities. It is virtually impossible to learn that emancipation for action to rectify one's impasse is available to the man who knows himself. What Ivan learns seems simple, but it is almost unattainable knowledge because society keeps one from seeing behind the protective coverings. Only Gerasim, the peasant who is untainted by education and cultural refinement, seems to know—a fact which has still other social implications.

Auerbach has suggested that nineteenth-century Russian fictional realism is unusual for its ability to regard "everyday things in a serious vein" because of the peculiar facts of Russian history. It is closer than Western realism to the old figural point of view: "it is based on a Christian and traditionally patriarchal concept of the creatural dignity of every human individual regardless of social rank and position . . ." (*Mimesis,* p. 460). This is surely true, and it is one of the factors which made it possible to conceive of salvation in the terms Tolstoy employed in *The Death of Ivan Ilyich*. Nevertheless, Tolstoy's attitude is not figural, for (more than his secularism) the isolation of Ivan Ilyich, as of all modern men, prevents him from seeing his life and suffering as fulfilling other events and as having a place in universal history. For him, it is enough to know "that it was possible to rectify all this" by one act of love. But it is impossible to place this observation into a meaningful and purposive historical continuum.

ALBERT CAMUS: THE PLAGUE

Albert Camus, in his novel *The Plague* (1947), resorted to allegory in order to depict the reactions of men of the twentieth century to the genocidal phenomena of the age. More particularly, he had in mind the men of the Resistance during the occupation of France in World War II. By choosing an outbreak of the bubonic plague as the symbol for total war and by using images of weather as a natural force beyond the control of men, he was able to emphasize the impotence of men to manipulate or resist the irrational in history. The book, then, deals with men faced with mass death and unable to extricate themselves from its terror.

If *The Plague* is to be called an allegory, it must be recognized that the term is being used in a rather special sense. Camus' device is to place his characters, men of the Resistance, in a symbolic setting. One expects that usually the characters in an allegory will be personifications of abstract moral qualities. The personages of this novel might be regarded as types, but there is nothing abstract about them. They are depicted as utterly ordinary men in the face of an extraordinary situation; their response is the subject of the work.

The device of allegory in this case might be defined as the sustained use of the plague as the setting for a novel which reflects upon World War II. Besides indicating Camus' feeling that genocidal war is beyond the normal resources which man usually employs in his efforts to direct and control history (a possibility which Camus regards as dubious even in less extreme instances), the symbolic setting has two effects. First, it gives the novelist distance from a historical event in which he himself was deeply involved and allows him to generalize the significance of the French Resistance. *The Plague,* thus, becomes not simply a novel of World War II but a novel of the twentieth-century experience and, indeed, of the human condition. It is an effort to relate present experience to a larger view of history and of man's role in history.

Furthermore, Camus is enabled by his allegorical device to portray the everyday experience of men in crisis. War is exceptional, cataclysmic, and the occasion for heroism in the conventions of the war novel until the time of Camus. The characters of war novels are too easily called upon for acts of bravado. By choosing as his narrator a physician who must day after day deal with the relentless destructiveness of the plague, but is little inclined to heroism or rationalization, the novelist is able to achieve a flatly matter-of-fact tone of reportage with very little rhetorical or histrionic embellishment. The very identity of Dr. Rieux as narrator is concealed until the end in order to avoid any temptation to depict his medical heroism; and Rieux stresses the fact that he is a writer of chronicle, not of hagiography or of historical interpretation. In the hands of a lesser writer, the tone might lapse into banality, but Camus remains firmly in control as he portrays the horror of the plague and its deadly reality.

The Plague is easily summarized. Residents of the coastal city of Oran in Algeria, about which "what strikes one first" is "its ordinariness," noticed one April in the 1940's that the rats were emerging from their hiding places to die grotesquely in the streets. Shortly later, citizens of Oran began to die of an incurable disease which, the medical community reluctantly acknowledged, was bubonic plague. A state of plague was proclaimed and the city closed. Throughout the summer and following winter, one observes the plague through the eyes of Dr. Rieux and his associates: an asthmatic who has utterly withdrawn from human intercourse; a civil clerk who has aspirations to write the perfect novel; a petty criminal who is reprieved from prosecution by the crisis of the plague; a journalist trapped by the plague in Oran who can think only of escaping to join his mistress in Paris but decides to remain once the opportunity to leave is offered; a priest; and Tarrou, the son of a French judge, who had fled his family when he discovered his father's role in the condemnation and execution of prisoners and, disenchanted with a political movement in which he had become involved because its order, too, "was based on the death sentence," devoted his life to "learning how to be a saint." As mysteriously and suddenly as it had come, the plague ultimately recedes.

Camus and his narrator, Rieux, never judge the motivations of the characters in *The Plague* or their right to respond as they wish to the disaster. One may, like the asthmatic, withdraw to an existence measured by moving chick peas from one container to another. The hedonism and opportunism of the majority of the citizens of Oran are duly recorded but not condemned. The greatest crisis for the characters is the death of a child who seems to them an innocent and helpless sufferer.

But in the course of the work, a general view which is heroic because of its very modesty gradually emerges. It is, simply, that one must respond to the needs of others in the face of a crisis which no one can control. Evil, as Tarrou says, "helps men to rise above themselves." By being a member of human society one is always at least a potential carrier of pestilence, of destructive evil. Thus, for Tarrou, although one may innocently become the means of the spread of death and evil, it is imperative that he not become a willing instrument in the dissemination of the plague. Sympathy seems to him the means to peace and, even, sainthood.

Rieux cannot share his friend's desire for sainthood, yet his view is similar. He learns "that there are more things to admire in men than to despise." But he also believes that there can be no complete victory over the plague and that one must strive to be a healer. The battle must be fought again and again.

As against the unassuming position of these men, which, despite themselves, is heroic, the view of the priest, Paneloux, seems fanatical as he moves from a prophetic announcement that the plague is a judgment on Oran to an assertion that men must accept the suffering which has been thrust upon them. Stricken himself, Paneloux becomes a passive martyr to the disease.

Death in *The Plague* is a phenomenon, a fact which is simply accepted. There is no hint of Mann's metaphysics; and nothing like Tolstoy's feeling that some sort of salvation can be worked out by means of self-realization. One simply does what one can—or, even, what he is moved to do—to combat the evil or absurdity which inevitably confronts anyone who exists in this world. This coming to terms with existence, with history or the plague, implies that facing death is a function of facing life. Rather one responds to the crisis put before him by the absurd in history. By so responding, he comes into contact with others, and a sense of community of purpose emerges. One learns "that there are more things to admire in men than to despise," and life assumes a minimal but sufficient purposiveness. Death can be endured and, in a sense, given a meaning which derives from life.

For Mann and Tolstoy the problematical nature of human character and the consequent isolation of man require that one deal as an individual with death and life. No one feels individual isolation more keenly than Camus, but the cataclysmic absurdity of twentieth-century existence has the effect of forcing men to turn to each other. The age of individualism has been followed by a period in which the manipulation of mass society has made the individual powerless to control and shape his existence. The idea that man shapes his society and thus progresses toward some sort of perfection is utterly bankrupt for Camus. But the point of view which emerges from *The Plague* is an anodyne for the loss of the idea of progress: it is no less than a rediscovery of the community of man. This new sense of community is both more poignant and more effective because of its lack of self-conscious heroism; men are knit together in the face of absurdity by their very refusal to surrender to the plague, and it is not the grand gesture which brings them together but the ordinary and seemingly insignificant.

Because of this sense of the importance of the mundane in the general human struggle, Camus recaptures in a peculiarly understated twentieth-century manner some of the characteristic notes of the earlier Christian figuralism. Faced with what are commonly called the apocalyptic or cataclysmic facts of life in this century, Camus is able to relate man's daily struggle with and for existence to a larger, historical struggle and, thus, to endow the struggle with a note of urgency.

But the abstractness of the allegorical setting, although it certainly does not tend toward the kind of denial of the reality of historical existence which characterized earlier allegorism, keeps Camus from appropriating the essential characteristic of figuralism: the relation of past events with present event within a purposive (but not necessarily progressive) continuum. Camus, of course, would not regard this as a flaw; nor would I contend that we should fault him, for this fact is simply to be regarded as an indication of the turn which the modern awareness of the problematic nature of existence and the isolation of men and events has taken in the perception of the writer. Life is purposive in that the community of men finds ways to cope with the absurd; but life is isolated in that there is no continuum within which the community of men can formulate the universal or historical significance of their experience in the face of death.

The modern novels discussed above suggest that there have been ways to talk about death in the modern period which have been more direct and more concerned with the mundane than many philosophical discussions. Even Mann's approach by way of the life of the soul displays a certain concern for everyday events as reflecting a spiritual reality. Tolstoy and Camus are able, because of their more direct concern with ordinary reality for its own sake and with the day-to-day events in the lives of their characters, to achieve a far greater impression of the relationship of man's death to his living. But all three novels demonstrate in varying degrees the isolation of modern man. He exists as a center of subjectivity observing and participating in events which are not part of a purposive continuum but are themselves isolated and self-contained. At the same time as the modern novel may show us ways to talk about death, then, it presents in a graphic and classical way the chief problem of man in the modern world: the fact that the individual is trapped by self and subjectivity.

2 INVOLVEMENT AND MORTALITY IN THE CONTEMPORARY WORLD

THE MODERN PERIOD is either ended, ending or undergoing a radical adjustment. It is too early to say whether a new mentality is emerging or whether we are now experiencing a radical fulfillment or implementation of the notions of freedom and toleration which were implicit in the rise of the empirical-experiential mode in the late-seventeenth century and toward which all of modern history has been tending. It is, however, clear that the international and domestic phenomena of this period require that theological reflection follow the lead of the late modern realistic novelists by taking more seriously the social nature and obligations of man.

Our age is, more clearly than even Camus could have seen after World War II, apocalyptic. Man is capable in the thermonuclear era of bringing upon himself the end of his worldly culture. But contemporary society is confronted by other phenomena, the manifestations of which are even more truly apocalyptic. In an unprecedented way, men are demanding the freedom and equality which are inherent in the doctrines of liberal democracy but which have always been denied through one sort or another of sophistry. Whether one thinks of nations, of races, or of economic groups, there is a confrontation of those possessed of the benefits of culture with the dispossessed which threatens to be cataclysmic, which quite transcends the power alignments of the modern period, and which is not ideological.

This latter characteristic is perhaps the most striking factor of the present situation. There have always been struggles in and among human societies. Many of them have been economically oriented as is the present struggle, but almost invariably their sources have been concealed behind ideologies. It is one of the few valid historical generalizations that, the more intense the ideological factors in human conflict, the more intense the physical struggle and the more excessive the retribution. One need only mention the Crusades and the French Revolution. The present, postmodern, and post-Cold War eruptions are, however, apparently not based upon systems of belief. Those who are confronting the establishments from the high school to the battlefield agree only that the common humanity of man has as its presupposition man's common freedom. That is an ideal in the most general sense; but, as the demand for implementation of that ideal is stated, it has no doctrinal content or program. Indeed, since these movements in our time have no system of belief or ideology, the establishments cannot cope with the situation because they are attuned to the modern experience of the confrontation of ideologies and the elaboration of balances of power.

The ramifications of the nonideological character of our age go even further, however. What has been substituted for systems of belief—for the content-orientation which has been typical of Western thought—is the need to be involved, immediately and directly, in whatever is at hand, be it a television program, a work of art, the act of love, or a protest. The consequences of this phenomenon for everything from matters of taste to matters of social policy are profoundly disturbing to most of us. But they are being worked out, usually without the awareness of the participants, in almost every area of life. One thinks of the preoccupation of contemporary literary criticism with form and rhetoric, of political concern with style to the virtual exclusion of issues, of the current faddism in fashion and the arts which have overturned all established notions of aesthetics. And one thinks of the demands for political and economic equality and acceptance which are not fettered by traditional considerations such as means of implementation or feasibility.

The need and demand for involvement is a key to understanding the remarkable present situation. It has, at least potentially, opened the way for contemporary man to escape from the isolation and autonomy imposed upon him by the mentality of the modern period. The demand for involvement is a demand that the age of anxiety and alienation be ended.

The problem of immortality versus resurrection, conceived as an ideological or doctrinal issue, is of little concern in the present situation. It may be that the issue of whether one can believe in either or should subscribe to either is an issue which Christians have argued long after either was compatible on a literal level with the empirical world-picture. The example of the modern novelists at least hints that one can speak of the meaning of death using some of the motifs of the Christian traditions without a commitment to their content.

Let us begin the effort to say something constructive about the problem of the meaning of our mortality, then, by admitting that, literally conceived, the idea of an afterlife has no place, makes no sense, and is inconsistent within the framework of the contemporary world-picture. It is still possible to produce massive rationalizations in an effort to devise a world-picture with room for either the immortality of the soul or the resurrection of the body, but such efforts always remain only rationalizations or endeavors to accommodate the picture of the past to the present. Christians should not try to force themselves to conceive what is inconceivable in their world.

But the issue raised by the conflict between immortality and resurrection has never been more crucial than it is at the present, even though we must speak of immortality and resurrection not as facts but as modes of approach to life. The issue is whether man should be and can be more interested in his subjective existence or in his social existence. The mode of resurrection calls upon man to live hard and well and boldly here and now and to understand that what he does is important in the historical continuum. The mode of immortality calls upon man to concern himself above all with his inner or mental or spiritual development and to regard his place in history as of secondary concern.

The issue, however, is still oversimplified if one thinks only in terms of a dichotomy between immortality and resurrection. Man's intellectual and reflective life—his concern with the processes of his salvation—is important to his well-being. The problem is that the mode of immortality tends to take the concern with the process and inner development as an end in itself. This cannot be, however, for—as the Greeks knew so well—man is an animal who lives in a *polis,* and the life of the mind cannot be separated from man's social being. The contemporary Gustave von Aschenbach must learn to relate his inner journey to the struggle of his society.

It is for this reason that one turns again to the figural attitude of the early and medieval Christians. It is not simplistically committed either to immortality or to resurrection. The way is not yet clear to a reconstruction of the sense of historical continuity and purposiveness which informed the figural method. Indeed, one of the most dangerous portents of our time is the threat that, as a function of the rejection of ideology, the historical point of view may be eclipsed. But the events of our times call urgently upon us to affirm that a radical love of life and the living constitutes the only chance for the survival of man and his cosmos. Thus, every gesture of every man affects his own fate and the fate of all men and has significance which belies its apparent insignificance. Life has a beginning and an ending. What stands between those poles affects not simply the individual but humanity.

Before the modern period, Christians used to keep before

themselves the fact of their mortality and to say to each other that, because man is mortal, every minute of every day is of crucial importance for the actor and for the rest of the people who are or will be the Kingdom of God. For this reason, they were not afraid to speak to each other of judgment; death is like the moment in court when all the evidence has been presented and one awaits the decision of judge and jury. Life is important and urgent because it is not everlasting. There are things to be done and little time is given us to do them. Indeed, the urgency is compounded by the fact that we do not know—even in an age of medically induced longevity—how little time there may be. *Memento mori:* "Remember, O Man, that dust thou art, and unto dust thou shalt return."

Christians before the modern period were not only preoccupied with the fact of death. They were also preoccupied with visions of the future. In the twentieth century, it is not possible to conceive of the future as they did; but it is necessary to keep constantly in mind the yearning for a transformed society and the possibility of its achievement. That hope, which Christians have called hope for the establishment of the Kingdom of God, is what makes possible and necessary the battle against death, the battle against absurdity. It makes mortal, and therefore urgent, life in the present a figure which gathers up even in its apparent insignificance and triviality all the aspirations of mortals of the past and all the potentialities of man's future.

One last caution must be entered. It is often alleged against preachers that when they exhort men to live well in the present, they are demanding an unreasonable kind of heroism which is not feasible for the little man. The point is well taken. "Urgency" has been a key concept in this essay. What should be remembered about the urgency of the figural approach, however, is that it invested the most common occurrences and the most humble people with significance. One has in mind not the martyrs but the Ivan Ilyich who understands at the very end of an utterly banal life and the characters of *The Plague* who respond so modestly to their crisis. One has in mind the Jewish rabbi who was physically afraid when he suffered an ignominious death by crucifixion, but whose death has been regarded by many as the basis for hope of the redemption and transformation of the world. To grasp this point about mortality, to which figuralism directs us, is to realize that we have been riding backward on the train.

This book began with an exploration of the manifestations of the helplessness and foolishness of modern man in the face of death. That essay was a picture of man without a rationale for death and, therefore, unable to face the fact of death. Perhaps it would be more accurate to say that late modern man's inability to cope with death is one more piece of evidence for the bankruptcy of ideology and the hard sell. We want an answer which is clear and simple—and which we simply cannot formulate. The picture of that essay, then, is a picture of an aspect of the social and intellectual sickness of late modern man.

The problem, however, is evanescent if it is correct that the solution lies not in a new or revived ideological formulation but in an attitude toward death which makes clear the importance of being involved in the world among men who are trying to fulfill the promise of a vision of the world transformed.

NOTES

PART I, CHAPTER 1 (pp. 2-18)

1. "Dulce Et Decorum Est" in C. Day Lewis, ed., *The Collected Poems of Wilfred Owen* (London: Chatto & Windus, 1963), p. 55.

2. "The Parable of the Old Man and the Young," *ibid.*, p. 42. Copyright, Chatto & Windus, Ltd., 1946, © 1963. Reprinted by permission of New Directions Publishing Corporation.

3. "Do not go gentle into that good night," in *The Collected Poems of Dylan Thomas* (New York: New Directions, 1957), p. 128. Copyright 1952 by Dylan Thomas. Reprinted by permission of New Directions Publishing Corporation.

4. New York: Simon and Schuster, 1963.

5. *Ibid.*, p. 77.

6. *Ibid.*, Chap. 13, *passim.*

7. The phrase was made famous in *Understanding Media* (New York: McGraw-Hill, 1964). The matter of funeral customs was discussed by McLuhan in *The Mechanical Bride: Folklore of Industrial Man* (New York: Vanguard Press, 1951), pp. 14-15.

8. But see her comments at pp. 190-191, 241-258.

9. New York: Avon Publishing Co., 1952. Although this novel of Huxley's is useful here, it may be observed that it is seriously flawed as a work of art by its needless and radical change of point of view and by the author's tedious use of William Propter as the mouthpiece for his own secularized and intellectualized mysticism.

10. *Ibid.*, p. 229.

11. At p. 39 (to cite only the first occurrence).

12. *Ibid.*, p. 350.

13. "Tithonus," line 70.

14. *Ibid.*, lines 1-10.

15. Garden City, New York: Doubleday, 1965.

16. Gorer, p. xiii.

17. *Ibid.*, pp. x-xi. As Miss Mitford points out (pp. 203-204), the American funeral industry is painfully aware of this phenomenon and almost evangelical in its zeal to reform Britain in this respect.

18. Gorer, pp. 24-43.

19. *Ibid.*, pp. 51-57.

20. *Ibid.*, p. 33.

21. *Ibid.*, 192-199 (reprinted from *Encounter,* October 1955).

22. *Mechanical Bride*, p. 15.

23. I derive the term and the definition from Robert N. Bellah's superb article, "Civil Religion in America," *Daedalus* (Journal of the American Academy of Arts and Sciences; Winter, 1967), pp. 1-21. Bellah traces the term to Rousseau and other figures like Franklin, who held "the existence of a Deity; that he made the world and govern'd it by his Providence; that the most acceptable service of God was the doing of good to men; that our souls are immortal; and that all crime will be punished, and virtue rewarded either here or hereafter." (*Autobiography*, as quoted by Bellah, p. 5).

24. New Haven: Yale University Press, 1961. The quotations that follow are used with permission. This volume is based on Warner's *The Living and the Dead* (1959), part of the Yankee City series in which Warner and colleagues conducted an extensive sociological analysis of a New England city. What follows is a summary of Part III, "The Living and the Dead."

25. *Ibid.*, pp. 161-162.

26. *Ibid.*, pp. 166-167.

27. *Ibid.*, p. 167.

28. *Ibid.*

29. *Ibid.*, pp. 200-201.

30. *Ibid.*, p. 207.

31. *Ibid.*, p. 209.

32. *Ibid.*, p. 211.

33. *Ibid.*, p. 212.

34. *Ibid.*, pp. 216-217.

35. *Ibid.*, p. 217. I have added a qualification to Warner to cover wars, like that in Vietnam, which fail to unify the people.

36. See Bellah, pp. 1-5.

37. The author attended the annual service commemorating "the Victory achieved in the Battle of Britain in the Year Nineteen Hundred and Forty" at Westminster Abbey in September, 1967. Although the Established Church had oversight of the proceedings,

they were essentially similar to those of an American civic memorial observance. The Abbey fulfills the function in Britain of the Arlington Cemetery and the Lincoln Memorial in America, but is particularly suitable to this occasion because of the presence there —in the eastern-most bay of the Chapel of Henry VII—of the memorial chapel and window of the Royal Air Force. At this service, the choir of the Abbey was occupied by the senior officers of the RAF, a representative of the Queen, and—perhaps most significant of all—Lady Clementine Spencer-Churchill. A large percentage of the congregation in the nave was made up of widows of those killed in the Battle, many of whom wore their husbands' ribbons and some of whom brought offerings of flowers to be placed before a memorial tablet in the cloister of the Abbey. A military band in the loft of the choir screen played symphonic selections before the service. The colors were placed upon the high altar during the playing of a trumpet fanfare, and the National Anthem was sung. Thus set, the service of Morning Prayer with added prayers remembering "our brothers who gave their lives that the many might live" became a poignant expression of the civic theology of meaningful, sacrificial death. The sermon by the Chaplain-in-Chief of the RAF could have been a Memorial Day sermon in America, urging the congregation to rededication to the kind of spirit which enabled those who died in the battle to make the ultimate sacrifice. The words of Winston Churchill ("Never in the field of human conflict was so much owed by so many to so few.") assume in this connection a function as sacred text comparable to that of the Gettysburg Address in American memorial rites. Appropriate bugle calls were sounded as the colors were removed from the altar, and the band played a RAF march as the dignitaries filed out of the church.

38. "Civil Religion in America," p. 16.

39. Svetlana Alliluyeva, *Twenty Letters to a Friend,* trans. Priscilla Johnson McMillan (New York: Harper & Row, 1967), pp. 9, 10.

40. Trans. Daphne Hardy (New York: Macmillan, 1963), p. 136.

41. *Death, Grief and Mourning,* p. 24.

42. "Immortality of the Soul or Resurrection of the Dead" (Ingersoll Lecture, 1955) in Krister Stendahl, ed., *Immortality and Resurrection* (New York: Macmillan, 1965), pp. 9-53. Reactions

to the first publication of the lecture in Europe are described in an "Afterword," pp. 47-53.

43. *The Family of God,* p. 233.

PART II, CHAPTER 1 (pp. 20-34)

1. Recent studies have stressed the possibility that Thucydides may not have written the oration until comparatively late in the process of sketching and revising his *History* and have tended to reassess the significance of Athenian imperialism in the light of the eclipse of modern imperialism. (For a good summary, see "The Periclean Dialogue," in *Times Literary Supplement,* No. 3338 [17 Feb. 1966], pp. 113-114.) Such problems—and those raised by the context of the speech—need not concern us here. No one in the present decade can fail to note (with the anonymous writer of the review cited) the "cold, smug, priggish quality about certain passages of the Funeral Oration which no amount of high idealism can wholly camouflage." Yet the Periclean oratory remains a great monument of Greek civic development and gives a particularly revealing glimpse of the official or political attitude toward death.

2. II. xli. 4–xliii. 1. The translation quoted is that of Charles Forester Smith in the Loeb Classical Library (rev. ed.; Cambridge: Harvard University Press, 1928), pp. 331-335.

3. See Jacqueline de Romilly, *Thucydides and Athenian Imperialism,* trans. Philip Thody (New York: Barnes & Noble, 1963), pp. 130-140 and 146-157.

4. The speech begins at II. xxxv and runs through xlvi.

5. On the use of this term and the problem of the Athenian custom of bringing the dead home for burial, see A. W. Gomme, *A Historical Commentary on Thucydides,* Vol. II (corrected printing; Oxford: Clarendon Press, 1962), pp. 94 ff.

6. II. xliii. 3.

7. Anonymous trans., quoted from Moses Hadas, ed., *The Greek Poets* (Modern Library; New York: Random House, 1953), p. 164.

8. Werner Jaeger, "The Greek Ideas of Immortality" (Ingersoll Lecture, 1958) in Stendahl, ed., *Immortality and Resurrection,* p. 101. Elsewhere (*Paideia: the Ideals of Greek Culture,* trans. Gilbert Highet, Vol. I [2nd ed.; New York: Oxford University Press, 1945], p. 411). Jaeger has spelled out the corollary of this notion: namely,

that because the Athenians, through their contributions to the state upon which their own immortality rests, serve as an example to the rest of Greek culture, the city too, has "the assurance of its own immortality."

9. Thucydides, II. lxiv. 6.

10. The correct interpretation of the Aristotelian dictum usually translated, "Man is a political animal." See H. D. F. Kitto, *The Greeks* (Harmondsworth: Penguin Books, 1951), p. 11.

11. *Phaedo,* 80c-81e. Trans. Hugh Tredennick, in Edith Hamilton and Huntington Cairns, eds., *The Collected Dialogues of Plato, Including the Letters* (Bollingen Series, LXXI; New York: Pantheon Books, 1961). Used with permission.

12. For a good discussion of the role of Socrates in the dialogues, see Paul Friedlaender, *Plato: An Introduction,* trans. Hans Meyerhoff (Bollingen Series, LIII; New York: Pantheon Books, 1958), pp. 12-20.

13. *Phaedo,* 63e-64a.

14. *Ibid.,* 64c.

15. *Ibid.,* 66d.

16. *Ibid.,* 67d.

17. *Ibid.,* 69c.

18. *Ibid.,* 70a.

19. *Ibid.,* 72e. For an extended demonstration of the doctrine of recollection, see the *Meno.*

20. *Phaedo,* 78d.

21. *Ibid.,* 81a.

22. *Ibid.,* 107c.

23. Jaeger in *Immortality and Resurrection,* pp. 102 ff, and *Paideia,* Vol. II (New York: Oxford University Press, 1943), *passim.*

24. *Republic,* 614b, ff.

25. Jaeger, *Paideia,* II, p. 367.

PART II, CHAPTER 2 (pp. 35-49)

1. On the biblical definition of History, see Lloyd G. Patterson, *God and History in Early Christian Thought* (Studies in Early Christian Thought; New York: Seabury Press, 1967), pp. 1-15.

2. For a survey of Old Testament attitudes toward death (with

which I disagree at several points), see Robert Martin-Achard, *From Death to Life: A Study of the Development of the Doctrine of the Resurrection in the Old Testament,* trans. John Penney Smith (Edinburgh: Oliver and Boyd, 1960).

3. Trans. E. A. Speiser ("The Anchor Bible," I; Garden City: Doubleday, 1964), p. 174. Used with permission. I am further indebted to Speiser's Introduction and Notes for helpful suggestions; to the Introduction and Commentary of C.A. Simpson in *The Interpreter's Bible,* I (Nashville: Abingdon Press, 1952); and to the articles of Edmond Jacob on "Death" and "Immortality" in *The Interpreter's Dictionary of the Bible* (Nashville: Abingdon Press, 1962). Lack of space has prevented me from taking account of the kinds of evidence presented by Roland de Vaux (*Ancient Israel: Its Life and Institutions,* trans. John McHugh [New York: McGraw-Hill, 1961], esp. at pp. 56-61); I am, however, convinced that these considerations do not fundamentally challenge my discussion.

4. Harvey H. Guthrie, Jr., *Wisdom and Canon: Meanings of the Law and the Prophets* (Winslow Lectures, 1966; Evanston: Seabury-Western Theological Seminary, 1966), pp. 4-5.

5. According to the Yahwist, who is not responsible for Gen. 25:1-11.

6. Here I go beyond other commentators, who are more cautious. The only other reference to this kind of oath is in Gen. 47:29; and it is, significantly, associated with the death of Israel, who is likewise preoccupied with thoughts of the land of the promise of Yahweh.

7. Because of the unique role of Abraham as the first patriarch, "in Abraham's bosom" became a common euphemism for death.

8. *Nephesh,* the Hebrew word which has often been translated "soul," means, rather, "that which is vital in man in the broadest sense" (Gerhard von Rad, *Old Testament Theology,* trans. D. M. G. Stalker [2 vols.; Edinburgh: Oliver and Boyd, 1962 and 1965], I, p. 153). Although *nephesh* is given to man at his creation and it returns to God at his death, the concept is closer to selfhood or life-force than to soul.

9. Guthrie, *Wisdom and Canon.* My statement of the themes of later Hebrew religious thought is heavily influenced by Guthrie in the work cited and in *God and History in the Old Testament* (New York: Seabury Press, 1960), pp. 117-137. See also von Rad, II, pp. 301-315. Not all scholars would agree to their formulation of

the relationship between Wisdom and apocalyptic, but it seems to me proper because of the essential contemporaneity of the traditions to see them as related rather than as antipathetic.

10. See von Rad, II, pp. 308-315.

11. I have not treated Wisdom of Solomon, which does incorporate the Hellenistic doctrine of the immortal soul into the Hebraic-historical framework, because of its late date (*c.* 100 B.C.-*c.* A.D. 40) and its uniqueness. Obviously, however, it shows the inherent possibilities of accommodation to Hellenism via the Wisdom tradition (and this is doubly significant in the light of its association with Alexandria where Christian philosophical theology was to flower) and represents a significant movement in late Judaism, the importance of which has only recently been recognized. One might argue that Wisdom only translates Hebraic notions into the Greek philosophical idiom (and I have been tempted to do so, claiming for the author a high level of sophistication and remarkable poetic powers); but in the light of the Christian history of the problem of immortality, that seems to be pushing things. It is easy to see why the Fathers were moved by this document. For further commentary, see Bruce C. Metzgar, *An Introduction to the Apocrypha* (New York: Oxford University Press, 1957), pp. 65-76.

12. My interpretation is heavily influenced by Oscar Cullmann's Ingersoll Lecture for 1955, "Immortality of the Soul or Resurrection of the Dead," reprinted in Stendahl, ed., *Immortality and Resurrection,* pp. 9-47; I go somewhat further than he, however.

13. See Dan. 12:5-13.

14. Werner Georg Kümmel, *Promise and Fulfillment: The Eschatological Message of Jesus,* trans. D. M. Barton ("Studies in Biblical Theology," 23; London: SCM Press, 1957), p. 153. See also Gunther Bornkamm, *Jesus of Nazareth,* trans. Irene and Fraser McLuskey with James M. Robinson (New York: Harpers, 1960), pp. 90-95.

15. See also Matt. 22:23-33.

16. See Joachim Jeremias, *The Parables of Jesus* (rev. ed.; London: SCM Press, 1963), *passim.*

17. Mark 13:5-37; Matt. 24:4-36; Luke 21:8-36.

18. See Kummel, *Promise and Fulfillment,* pp. 88 ff.

19. See Cullmann in *Immortality and Resurrection,* pp. 12-20

20. Regretfully, considerations of length prevent us from dealing here with the John Gospel, for it has seemed to many to represent a Hellenized point of view. Despite its radically different vocabulary,

I regard it more and more as a document in which Hellenic terms are used to present Hebraic notions. Its real sources lie in the Wisdom movement; but its exegetical interpretation has been shaped by the Alexandrian philosophical theologians.

21. Paul's writing, of course, antedates that of the Evangelists and in some ways influences them. The present order of discussion is based on the assumption that Mark 12:18 ff. is a comparatively untouched *logion*. The signs of the Synoptic Apocalypse are not free from later influences, and even the reference therein to the resurrection may not be authentic.

22. Paul treats this problem more directly in I Thess. 4:13-18.

23. See Part I, Chapter 1, note 41.

PART II, CHAPTER 3 (pp. 50-63)

1. The methodology I have adopted in this study has forced me to overlook or to oversimplify a number of the developments in philosophy between Plato and the Fathers. I trust, however, it will be clear that those developments were considerable and important and that when the Fathers spoke of Platonism they referred not so much to the teaching of the author of the dialogues as to the thought of the more recent interpreters of Plato. It ought in particular to be noted here that the Fathers' grappling with the problem of immortality should not be seen against the background of Plato's own dialogues but as a contribution to the Hellenistic discussion of the immortality of the soul, in which the issue as to whether the soul was or was not created was central. The Fathers had, on the whole and for obvious reasons, to deny that possibility and, thus, even to enhance the importance of the issue. For the relationship of the Fathers to Hellenistic philosophy with special reference to the doctrine of the soul see, for example, Richard A. Norris, Jr., *Manhood and Christ: A Study in the Christology of Theodore of Mopsuestia* (Oxford: Clarendon Press, 1963), Part I, especially chap. 3, and John M. Rist, *Eros and Psyche: Studies in Plato, Plotinus, and Origen* (*Phoenix,* Supplementary Vol. VI; Toronto: University of Toronto Press, 1964).

2. Two important studies which probe this interpretation of the origins of Gnosticism are R. McL. Wilson, *The Gnostic Problem: A Study of the Relations between Hellenistic Judaism and the Gnostic Heresy* (London: Mowbray, 1958), and R. M. Grant,

Gnosticism and Early Christianity (New York: Columbia University Press, 1959).

3. Grant, p. 38.

4. The language of the Western Church was at first Greek, and it remained so in Rome for a remarkably long time. The first Latin Christian literature appeared in Africa in the second century, and the growth of the intellectual cleavage between East and West can be followed in part by tracing the rise of Latin as a second Christian language within the Empire.

5. *Against Heresies* V. xxxi. 2. Trans. quoted from *The Ante-Nicene Fathers,* Vol. I (reprint of the 1885 ed.; Grand Rapids: Eerdmans, 1956).

6. *Against Heresies* II. xxxiii.

7. *Ibid.,* II. xxxiv. 1.

8. *Ibid.,* V. vi. 1. Irenaeus is here attacking the Gnostic idea that the physical body is not essential to man but a prison for the essential soul. He relies heavily upon the allusion in I Thess. 5:23 in which body, soul, and spirit are linked in a (liturgical?) formula. The passage is a unique one in Paul and probably does not reflect his acceptance of the common Hellenistic philosophical anthropology. In view of the fact that the passage is part of the doxology of the letter, it is dangerous to put too much weight on it, though Irenaeus is hardly alone in this regard (see John A. T. Robinson, *The Body: A Study in Pauline Theology* [Studies in Biblical Theology, 5; London: SCM Press, 1952], pp. 27 and 17n).

9. *Against Heresies* V. vi. 1. ("But if the Spirit be wanting to the soul, he who is such is indeed of an animal nature, and being left carnal, shall be an imperfect being, possessing indeed the image [of God] in his formation . . . , but not receiving the similitude through the Spirit. . . .")

10. *Ibid.,* V. vii. 1.

11. *Ibid.,* V. xxxiv. 1. (". . . each class [of souls] receives a habitation such as it has deserved, even before the judgment.")

12. *On the Theology of Death,* trans. C. H. Henkey (Quaestiones Disputatae; New York: Herder and Herder, 1961), p. 24.

13. For an excellent general sketch, on which I rely for this account of Origen's background and place in Alexandrian intellectual life, see Hans von Campenhausen, *The Fathers of the Greek Church,* trans. Stanley Godman (New York: Pantheon, 1959), pp. 40-56.

14. For a lucid exposition of the cosmological background of

Origen's system, see R. A. Norris, Jr., *God and World in Early Christian Theology* (Studies in Patristic Thought; New York: Seabury Press, 1965), pp. 129-157. See also E. R. Dodds, *Pagan and Christian in an Age of Anxiety* (Cambridge: Cambridge University Press, 1965), pp. 127-130.

15. *Contra Celsum* V. 23. Trans. quoted from Henry Chadwick, *Origen: Contra Celsum* (corrected reprint; Cambridge: Cambridge University Press, 1956). Used with permission. Chadwick italicizes Origen's quotations from Celsus.

16. See Werner Jaeger, *Early Christianity and Greek Paideia* (Cambridge: Harvard University Press, 1961), p. 66.

17. *Contra Celsum* V. 14-17. Origen's teaching in this regard is often interpreted as foreshadowing (or espousing) the doctrine of purgatory. It is, however, very far from the Western doctrine. These references to fire are actually metaphoric for the purification of the soul and not descriptions of a state in which the soul is punished for its earthly misdemeanors.

18. Campenhausen (p. 16) rightly remarks that "The fact that Origen transgresses the frontiers of the Christian revelation shows that he is aware that all his speculations are inevitably marked by an element of metaphor and poetry. But he does not doubt that in this way he approaches more closely to the truth contained in the Bible than he would if he simply kept to the literal 'disguised' assertions of its anthropomorphism as the simple unphilosophical mass of the faithful are in the habit of doing."

19. L. G. Patterson, 'The Conversion of *Diastēma* in the Patristic View of Time," in R. A. Norris, Jr., ed., *Lux in Lumine: Essays to Honor W. Norman Pittenger* (New York: Seabury Press, 1966), p. 105.

20. *On the Soul and the Resurrection* in "Nicene and Post-Nicene Fathers," Second Series, Vol. V, ed. and trans. William More and Henry Austin Wilson (Grand Rapids: Eerdmans, n.d. [reprint of 1892 ed.]), p. 438. Subsequent citations are to this volume by page and column.

21. *Ibid.*, p. 433b.

22. *Ibid.*

23. *Ibid.*, p. 433a.

24. *Ibid.*, p. 437b.

25. *Ibid.*, p. 442a.

26. *Ibid.*, p. 443b.

27. *Ibid.*, pp. 445-446.

28. *Ibid.*, pp. 446-448.

29. *Ibid.*, pp. 448-453.

30. *Ibid.*, pp. 453b-459.

31. *Ibid.*, pp. 460-468.

32. See Campenhausen, p. 109.

33. *Phaedo* 114b. See also Friedlaender, *Plato: An Introduction*, chap. IX.

34. On Gregory's teaching as a refutation of Origen, see J. Daniélou, "La Résurrection des Corps chez Grégoire de Nysse," *Vigiliae Christianae,* VII (1953), pp. 154-170, at pp. 154-155.

PART II, CHAPTER 4 (pp. 64-78)

1. Plato, *Republic* 614b-621.

2. Cicero, *Republic* VI. x-xxvi.

3. *On the Resurrection of the Flesh* XIV, XVII. The trans. quoted is that of Peter Holmes in *Ante-Nicene Fathers,* III, pp. 546-595. See also *A Treatise on the Soul,* at pp. 181-235, which must be read with *Resurrection. On the Soul* is probably from the Montanist period of Tertullian's career (see Johannes Quasten, *Patrology,* Vol. II [Westminster, Md.: Newman Press, 1958], pp. 287-289); it seems to me the less representative of the tone of the corpus of Tertullian.

4. *Resurrection* XI.

5. W. H. C. Frend, *Martyrdom and Persecution in the Early Church* (Oxford: Basil Blackwell, 1965), points out that "just when the East was substituting a metaphysical for an apocalyptic view of Christianity, Tertullian was opening his defence of the faith in Carthage with a vindication of the open profession of the Name and the goal of martyrdom" (p. 348). He sees this metaphysical-apocalyptic division as one of the chief sources of divergent theological tendencies in East and West.

6. *Resurrection* XVII.

7. On the difficulties, see Norris, *God and World,* pp. 112-113.

8. See *On the Soul* LI-LVIII.

9. The case of the souls of the martyrs is different (and here Tertullian sets a course generally followed by the early Fathers), for they are granted immediate entrance into Paradise (*e.g., On the Soul* LV: "The sole key to unlock Paradise is your own life's blood").

10. *On the Soul* LVI.
11. *Resurrection* LVII-LXII.
12. *Ibid.,* XIV.
13. *Ibid.,* VIII.
14. I am especially aware that in this and the preceding chapter —but most especially with Augustine—I have had to gloss over the complex problem of time as it is related to the picture of salvation and the destiny of the soul. I can only quote briefly here the useful article by Professor Patterson in *Lux in Lumine* and hope that my argument does not do violence to these crucial matters: "For . . . the Cappadocians time and motion remain fundamentally unfortunate characteristics of cosmic existence, but for Augustine it is the sinful distraction of the soul by the successiveness of life which is the real misfortune; and for him redemption lies not in the eventual emergence of the soul beyond time and change as such but in the redirection of the will away from this life toward that offered by God" (p. 109).
15. *Enchiridion* 109 and 111. Trans. quoted from Albert C. Outler, *Augustine: Confessions and Enchiridion* (Library of Christian Classics, VII; Philadelphia: Westminster Press, 1955), pp. 337-412. Used with permission.
16. *Enchiridion* 68.
17. *Ibid.,* 69. See also *City of God* XXI. 13. It should be noted here that Augustine accepts without question the cult of the martyrs and the practice of prayer for the dead (*e.g., Enchiridion* 110) but insists that the latter custom is meritorious only for the elect. He also insists that the vision of God is reserved until after the resurrection (see F. van der Meer, *Augustine the Bishop,* trans. B. Battershaw and G. R. Lamb [New York: Sheed and Ward, 1961], pp. 471-474).
18. So, to take a very recent case, A. C. Rush in the article on Gregory in *New Catholic Encyclopedia,* Vol. VI (New York, 1967). My own views on the subject are expounded more completely in a paper read at the Conference on Patristic Studies (Oxford, 1967) and to be published in *Studia Patristica.*
19. *Dialogues* IV. 41. Trans. quoted from Odo John Zimmerman, *Saint Gregory the Great, Dialogues* (Fathers of the Church, 39; New York: Fathers of the Church, Inc., 1959). Used with permission.
20. *Dialogues* I. Pref.
21. The best analysis of Gregory's contemplative piety is still

Cuthbert Butler, *Western Mysticism,* 2nd ed. (1922; reprinted as a Harper Torchbook; New York: Harpers, 1966), pp. 65-92 and 171-188.

22. *Dialogues* IV. 15, 16, 17, 20, 28, 40.

23. *Ibid.,* III. 38.

24. *Ibid.,* IV. 1.

25. *Ibid.,* III. 38.

26. *Ibid.,* IV. 43.

27. On the role of the *Dialogues* in the development of Gregory's reputation, see Henri de Lubac, *Exégèse Médiévale: Les Quatre Sens de l'Ecriture,* Vol. I. 2 (Paris: Aubier, 1959), p. 537.

28. *Dialogues* IV. 26. For this reason I regard as excessive some of the claims made by Joseph P. McClain in *The Doctrine of Heaven in the Writings of Saint Gregory the Great* (Studies in Sacred Theology, 2nd Ser., Vol. 95; Washington: Catholic University Press, 1956). McClain's evidence is largely from the *Moralia in Job* which is a transcription of exegetical lectures addressed to monks and does not always make clear the distinction between the rewards of the ascetics and of men in general.

PART II, CHAPTER 5 (pp. 79-93)

1. See Jean Leclercq, *The Love of Learning and the Desire for God: A Study of Monastic Culture,* trans. C. Misrahi (New York: Mentor-Omega, 1962), Part II.

2. See R. W. Southern, *The Making of the Middle Ages* (London: Hutchinson, 1953), pp. 234-235.

3. *E.g.,* Tertullian, *On the Resurrection of the Flesh* XII.

4. J. E. Cross, "The Conception of the Old English *Phoenix,*" in Robert P. Creed, ed., *Old English Poetry: Fifteen Essays* (Providence: Brown University Press, 1967), pp. 129-152 at pp. 137-138. My interpretation is strongly influenced by that of Cross, though hereafter I acknowledge only direct instances of indebtedness. For the Old English text and general suggestions from introduction and notes, I am indebted to N. F. Blake, ed., *The Phoenix* (Old and Middle English Texts; Manchester: University Press, 1964). Blake also prints the Latin of Lactantius and other texts related to the poem.

5. There is no single source for this part of the poem, but it reflects a wide acquaintance with patristic literature (see Blake, pp. 17-24).

6. *Phoenix,* lines 482-517; trans. mine. Complete trans. available in R. K. Gordon, *Anglo-Saxon Poetry* (Everyman's Library, 794; New York: Dutton, 1962), pp. 239-251.

7. Lines 92a, 117b, 183a, 208b, 289a. See Cross, p. 142.

8. See Ernst Robert Curtius, *European Literature and the Latin Middle Ages,* trans. Willard R. Trask (Bollingen Series, XXXVI; New York: Pantheon Books, 1953), pp. 17-71. The use of *topoi* or "topics" in medieval literature is of utmost importance for understanding the nature of the art of composition.

9. Blake, pp. 25-29.

10. Cross, p. 142. Cross's thesis is that *Phoenix* follows the fourfold pattern of biblical exegesis. His argument is compelling, but I am not convinced that the use of exegetical technique here is conscious.

11. *Phoenix,* lines 424-481.

12. Text in George Philip Krapp and Elliott van Kirk Dobbie, eds., *The Anglo-Saxon Poetic Records,* Vol. III (New York: Columbia University Press, 1936), pp. 174-178. A longer version with numerous variants and the speech of the righteous soul to its body appears in the Vercelli book (*ibid.,* Vol. II [1932], pp. 54-59). I have considered the prose versions in "Two Uses of Apocrypha in Old English Homilies," *Church History,* XXXIII (1964), pp. 379-391.

13. Trans. available in Edgar Hennecke, *New Testament Apocrypha,* ed. Wilhelm Schneemelcher, trans. R. McL. Wilson, Vol. II (Philadelphia: Westminster Press, 1965), pp. 755-798.

14. *Soul and Body* (Exeter), lines 71-96; trans. mine. Trans. of the Vercelli text is available in Gordon, *Anglo-Saxon Poetry,* pp. 280-283.

15. Stanley B. Greenfield, *A Critical History of Old English Literature* (New York: New York University Press, 1965), p. 180.

16. This is not always the case when the *topos* is employed, but, as I have suggested in the article cited above, there seems to be a tendency in the Old English period to relate—or actually to associate—the souls' addresses to the judgment.

17. For an excellent discussion of Aelfric's style and methodology, see Peter Clemoes, "Aelfric," in E. G. Stanley, ed., *Continuations and Beginnings: Studies in Old English Literature* (London: Nelson, 1966), pp. 176-209.

18. Printed in Migne, *Patrologia Latina,* Vol. XCVI, 461-524.

19. Enid M. Raynes, "MS. Boulogne-sur-Mer 63 and Aelfric," *Medium Aevum,* XXVI (1957), pp. 65-73.

20. John C. Pope, *Homilies of Aelfric, A Supplementary Collection. . . ,* Vol. I (Early English Text Society, No. 259; London: Oxford University Press, 1967), p. 407.

21. *Sermo ad Populum,* lines 94-215, 216-272 and 273-574, respectively, in Pope's ed., pp. 415-447. Hereafter cited simply by line number.

22. Lines 181-199; trans. mine.

23. Lines 545-574; trans. mine.

24. Neither Aelfric nor his source uses the word "purgatory" for the middle condition, though both speak of "hell" and "heaven" and treat "rest" as a metaphor for being in heaven. The thirteenth-century glossator of Pope's MS. R treats several of Aelfric's English words as synonymous with the purgatorial concepts of his own age.

25. *Sermo ad Populum,* lines 216-218.

26. Lines 259-260.

27. There is one exemplum, lines 168-176, which is similar to Gregory's wonder tales. It was added by Aelfric to his source material, but does not significantly alter the course of his argument. Its source is unknown.

28. David Knowles, *The Evolution of Medieval Thought* (London: Longmans, 1962), p. 75.

PART II, CHAPTER 6 (pp. 94-111)

1. Southern, *Making of the Middle Ages,* pp. 234-236 and 170-184. For further comment on Anselm and the revival of dialectics, see Knowles, *Evolution of Medieval Thought,* 93-106.

2. Southern, pp. 219-257.

3. "Shroud and Grave," No. 20 in Carleton Brown, ed., *English Lyrics of the XIIIth Century* (Oxford: Clarendon Press, 1932). See also Nos. 28 ("Doomsday") and 29 ("The Latemast Day") in both of which the new individualism and piety also tend to break through.

4. M. D. Chenu, *Toward Understanding Saint Thomas,* trans. with authorized corrections and bibliographical additions by A. M. Landry and D. Hughes (Chicago: Henry Regnery, 1964), pp. 289-292.

5. *Summa Contra Gentiles* IV. 91. 4, 6. Trans. quoted from *On the Truth of the Catholic Faith: Summa Contra Gentiles,* trans. A. C. Pegis (Bk. I), J. F. Anderson (Bk. II), V. J. Bourke (Bk. III), and C. J. O'Neil (Bk. IV) (Image Books, D26-D29; Garden City: Doubleday, 1955-1957). Used with permission.

6. Knowles, *Evolution of Medieval Thought,* p. 295; see also pp. 291-296. For Aristotle, the soul is the form of the body, and there is less emphasis upon the possibility of its independent existence than there had been in Plato.

7. *Contra Gentiles* IV. 56. 7.

8. *Ibid.,* IV. 79-97.

9. *Ibid.,* IV. 79. 3-4.

10. *Ibid.,* IV. 79. 10. These assertions are explicitly related to the philosophical proof of immortality in Bk. III.

11. *Ibid.,* IV. 79. 11.

12. *Ibid.,* IV. 79. 12.

13. *Ibid.,* IV. 82, 84-85.

14. *Ibid.,* IV. 91. 2. See also III. 51.

15. *Ibid.,* IV. 72. 14.

16. *Ibid.,* IV. 91. 7.

17. *Ibid.,* IV. 92-95.

18. *Ibid.,* IV. 96. 1.

19. Thomas's disciples who completed *Summa Theologiae* (III. a Suppl. Q. 88.2) come closer to this position than Thomas himself.

20. See John T. McNeill, *A History of the Cure of Souls* (Harper Torchbooks, TB 126; New York: Harpers, 1965), Chap. VI, *passim.*

21. This is not to say that Dante is a Thomist but that he knew and reflected the construct of the schoolmen. See Étienne Gilson, *Dante and Philosophy,* trans. David Moore (Harper Torchbooks, TB 1089; New York: Harpers, 1963), and Curtius, *European Literature,* pp. 223-225 and 372.

22. *Purgatorio* XXV. 22-27. Bernard Stambler, *Dante's Other World: The "Purgatorio" as a Guide to the "Divine Comedy"* (New York: New York University Press, 1957), pp. 218-219.

23. *Purgatorio* XXV. 32. Trans. quoted from Dante Alighieri, *The Purgatorio,* trans. John Ciardi with intro. by Archibald T. Macallister (Mentor Classic; New York: New American Library, 1961). Quoted matter that follows is used with permission. For the Italian text, I have used the 3 vol. ed. with trans. of John D. Sinclair (Galaxy Books, 65-67; New York: Oxford University Press, 1961).

Ciardi (p. 259) regards Virgil's deference to Statius as a matter of courtesy and not of doctrine. But according to Gilson (pp. 124-125), Dante, in *Banquet,* differs from the Thomists as to whether immortality is a matter of faith or reason, and this passage must be interpreted as an assertion that only "faith makes us perfectly sure" of immortality.

24. *Purgatorio* XXV. 34-78.

25. *Purgatorio* XXV. 79-108.

26. *Purgatorio* XXV. 77-78. See Ciardi's notes and (for the Averroists) Knowles, *Evolution of Medieval Thought,* pp. 200-201 and 272-275.

27. *I.e.,* in *Banquet.* See Gilson, *Dante and Philosophy,* pp. 124-125. Erich Auerbach (*Dante: Poet of the Secular World,* trans. Ralph Manheim [1929; Chicago: University of Chicago Press, 1961], p. 87) regards this as "perhaps Dante's most serious deviation from dogma" and discusses the aesthetic relationship to the *Aeneid.*

28. *Paradiso* XXV. 88-135. All three books of the *Comedy* have discussions of the nature of post-mortem existence in their twenty-fifth cantos. In *Inferno* the metamorphoses of thieves are described.

29. *Inferno* VI. 94-111.

30. Auerbach, *Dante,* p. 133.

31. See Morton W. Bloomfield, *Piers Plowman as a Fourteenth Century Apocalypse* (New Brunswick: Rutgers University Press, n.d. [1963]), p. 173. It is Bloomfield's thesis that the poem reflects primarily not the scholastic intellectual tradition but that of medieval monasticism as mediated with significant changes by St. Bernard and Joachim of Flora and by the continuing monastic tradition. I have some reservations about the formulation of the thesis; but Bloomfield is surely correct in general, and his book has been very helpful to me in formulating these comments on the poem.

32. *Piers Plowman, B*-text, X. 399-421. My trans. from Walter W. Skeat, ed., *The Vision of William Concerning Piers the Plowman. . . .*, 2 vols. (London: Oxford University Press, 1961 [ed., of 1886, reprinted with bibliography]). There is a complete trans. of the *B*-version by J. F. Goodridge (Penguin Classics; Baltimore: Penguin Books, 1959); the recent ed. of portions of the *C*-text by Elizabeth Salter and Derek Pearsall (York Medieval Texts; Evanston: Northwestern University Press, 1967) has an excellent introduction.

33. *Piers Plowman* I. 11-19.

34. Bloomfield, *Piers,* chap. IV. Dante's purgatory is a condition in time and conceived as being physically between heaven and hell; but Dante is dealing within an utterly different kind of visionary framework in which only his figuralism enables him to treat the historical seriously. Langland, in his similarly patterned but more earthbound vision, cannot (and does not want to) achieve the same kinds of abstractness and universality.

35. Bloomfield, pp. 123-124. Langland is probably influenced in

this regard by Joachim of Flora's apocalyptic notion of an age of the Holy Spirit which is about to come into being. But the hour of man's salvation for Langland is the Harrowing of Hell (*B*-text, Passus XVIII), which is described in precisely the terms criticized by Anselm.

36. Bloomfield, p. 165.

37. *Ibid.,* pp. 115-130. *B*-text VII. 108-115 and XIX. 177-193.

38. *C*-text VI. 1-104, esp. lines 45 ff. See also E. Talbot Donaldson, *Piers Plowman: The C-Text and Its Poet* (reprinted with new preface; Hamden: Archon Books, 1966), pp. 199-226.

39. Donaldson, pp. 188-193, 196-197.

40. Bloomfield, p. 64.

41. For a good survey, handsomely illustrated, see T. S. R. Boase, "King Death: Mortality, Judgment and Remembrance," in Joan Evans, *The Flowering of the Middle Ages* (London: Thames and Hudson, 1966), pp. 203-244.

42. John XXII (1316-1334) preached sermons in 1331-1332 arguing that the saints must await the resurrection for the beatific vision, and the damned the same event before entering hell. He did not argue against immortality, but felt that the separated soul could know only Christ's humanity. John's Franciscan enemies were particularly violent in their reaction to the "heresy." John reaffirmed his orthodoxy in 1334: "We confess and believe that souls separated from their bodies and fully purged from guilt are above, in the kingdom of heaven, in paradise and with Jesus Christ, in the company of the angels, and that according to the universal law, they see God and the divine essence face to face and clearly, *so far as the state and condition of a separated soul permits*" (quoted from G. Mollat, *The Popes at Avignon: 1305-1378* [Harper Torchbooks, TB 308; New York: Harpers, 1963], p. 23).

PART II, CHAPTER 7 (pp. 112-128)

1. Florence, Session VI; text in Centro di Documentazione-Bologna, ed., *Conciliorum Oecumenicorum Decreta* (Freiburg: Herder, 1962), pp. 503, line 30-504, line 14. The position of Roman Catholic orthodoxy is, from this period, fixed in its adherence to the kind of view of death and the afterlife represented by Aquinas. For this reason, I have felt free to deal exclusively with Protestant figures in this chapter, although the Counter Reformation position ought properly to be discussed.

2. Notably Heiko Obermann in *The Harvest of Medieval Theology: Gabriel Biel and Late Medieval Nominalism* (Cambridge: Harvard University Press, 1963).

3. Luther, Tischreden III. 3695 (Weimar Ausgabe, 1914). Trans. of the Latin version. Luther's comments on eschatological matters are widely scattered; for, as Paul Althaus remarks (*Die Theologie Martin Luthers* [Guetersloh: Mohn, 1962], p. 339), his eschatological views are tied inextricably to his *theologia crucis*. Hugh Thomson Kerr, Jr., ed., *A Compend of Luther's Theology* (Philadelphia: Westminster Press, 1943), has a representative collection of comments in translation; and the summary of Althaus, pp. 339-354, is reliable. In addition to the citations below, see the Commentary on Psalm 90 (in vol. XIII of J. Pelikan and H. T. Lehman, eds. *Luther's Works, American Edition* [Philadelphia and St. Louis, 1955, sqq.], pp. 73-141).

4. "Defense and Explanation of All the Articles," *Luther's Works, American Edition,* XXXII, p. 98.

5. See esp. Nos. 8, 10, 11, 15-17, 27, 82 (in Henry Bettenson, ed., *Documents of the Christian Church* [2nd ed; New York: Oxford University Press, 1963], pp. 260-268). Nos. 15-17 seem to foreshadow Luther's later position of purgatory.

6. Letter to Bartholomew von Staremberg (1524) in T. G. Tappert, ed., *Luther: Letters of Spiritual Counsel* (Library of Christian Classics [hereafter cited L.C.C.], XVIII; Philadelphia: Westminster Press, 1953, sqq.), p. 54.

7. Letter to Thomas Zink (1532), L.C.C., XVIII, p. 65.

8. W. Pauck, ed., *Luther: Lectures on Romans,* L.C.C., XV, p. 181.

9. *Ibid.,* p. 179.

10. See B. A. Gerrish, *Grace and Reason: A Study in the Theology of Luther* (Oxford: Clarendon Press, 1962), Chap. 2 and pp. 168-169.

11. "To the Christian Nobility of the German Nation," in *Works of Martin Luther* (Philadelphia Edition, Vol. II; Philadelphia: Muhlenberg Press, 1943), p. 146.

12. *Ibid.,* p. 147.

13. All citations are to the ed. of J. T. McNeill, trans. F. L. Battles in L.C.C., XX-XXI. Used with permission. For a reliable secondary survey, see Heinrich Quistorp, *Calvin's Doctrine of the Last Things,* trans. H. Knight (London: Lutterworth Press, 1955).

14. *Institutes* III. xxv. 6.

15. *Ibid.,* III. iii. 8.

16. *Ibid.,* III. iii. 17.

17. *Ibid.,* III. iv. 3.
18. *Ibid.,* III. iv, *passim.,* and IV. xii. See alseo McNeill, *History of the Cure of Souls,* pp. 197-200.
19. *Institutes* III. iv. 25-27.
20. *Ibid.,* III. v. 3.
21. *Ibid.,* III. v. 6.
22. *Ibid.,* III. v. 7-9.
23. *Ibid.,* III. v. 10.
24. *Ibid.,* I. xv. 2.
25. *Ibid.,* I. xv. 3.
26. *Ibid.,* I. xv. 6.
27. *Ibid.,* III. ix. 1.
28. *Ibid.,* III. ix. 4.
29. *Ibid.,* III. ix. 5-6.
30. *Ibid.,* III. xi-xxiv.
31. *Ibid.,* III. xxv. 1-5.
32. *Ibid.,* III. xxv. 6, and nn. 12-13.
33. "Hamlet: The Prince or The Poem?" *Proceedings of the British Academy,* XXVIII (1942), pp. 139-154, at p. 149.
34. *Hamlet* I. v. 9-22. The text used is that of George Lyman Kittredge in *The Complete Works of Shakespeare* (Boston: Ginn, 1936).
35. *Hamlet* III. i. 78-83.
36. *Hamlet* V. ii. 231-234. Maynard Mack in "The World of *Hamlet," The Yale Review,* XLI (1952), pp. 502-523, argues convincingly that Hamlet's change of attitude is first seen in the graveyard scene where "he confronts, recognizes, and accepts the condition of being man" (p. 522).
37. Quotations from *The First and Second Prayer Books of Edward VI,* intro. by E. C. S. Gibson (Everyman's Library, 448; New York: Dutton, 1957), pp. 269-277 and 424-427. See also Francis Procter and Walter Howard Frere, *A New History of the Book of Common Prayer . . .* (4th rev. ed.; London: Macmillan, 1955), pp. 630-638 and 644.
38. "This is my playes last scene . . . ," lines 5-6. Donne quotations are all from Herbert J. C. Grierson, ed., *Metaphysical Lyrics and Poems of the Seventeenth Century: Donne to Butler* (Oxford: Clarendon Press, 1921). I owe the suggestion of the relevance of Donne's sleep images to Professor William Williams of Northern Illinois University.
39. "Death be not proud . . . ," line 8.

40. "Song," lines 1-8.
41. *Ibid.,* lines 29-32.
42. *Ibid.,* lines 33-40.

PART III, CHAPTER 2 (pp. 136-158)

1. For the first two of these positions, see the articles of Oscar Cullmann and Harry A. Wolfson in Stendahl, ed., *Immortality and Resurrection,* pp. 9-53 and 54-96. The third position is ably defended by Jaroslav Pelikan, *The Shape of Death: Life, Death and Immortality in the Early Fathers* (New York: Abingdon Press, 1961), pp. 33-34.
2. For a good discussion of the problem of cosmology in classical philosophy, see R. A. Norris, Jr., *God and World in Early Christian Theology,* chap. I
3. David Knowles, *Evolution of Medieval Thought,* p. 7.
4. See E. R. Dodds, *Pagan and Christian in an Age of Anxiety,* chap. I.
5. *Ibid.,* p. 11; Werner Jaeger, *Early Christianity and Greek Paideia,* p. 90.
6. See Geoffrey Gorer, *Death, Grief and Mourning,* pp. 51-57. An acceptance of parapsychological phenomena seems to have influenced James A. Pike's recent defense of immortality in chap. VII of *If This Be Heresy* (New York: Harpers, 1967).
7. Dodds, *Pagan and Christian,* pp. 38-39.
8. *On the Soul* XLIII (*Ante-Nicene Fathers,* III).
9. *Ibid.,* XLV.
10. *Ibid.,* XLVII.
11. Macrobius, *Commentary on the Dream of Scipio,* trans. with intro. and notes by William Harris Stahl (Records of Civilization, Sources and Studies, XLVIII; New York: Columbia University Press, 1966).
12. See Stahl's introduction, pp. 23-39.
13. *Ibid.,* p. 13.
14. Macrobius, *Commentary* I. i. 7-8.
15. *Ibid.,* I. ii. 9.
16. *Ibid.,* I. ii. 13.
17. *Ibid.,* I. ii. 13.
18. *Ibid.,* I. iii. 2.
19. *Ibid.,* I. iii. 7.
20. *Ibid.,* I. iii. 10.

21. *Ibid.*, I. iii. 18.
22. *Dialogues* IV. 1.
23. *Ibid.*, IV. 50.
24. *Moralia* VIII. xxiv. 41 (*Patrologia Latina* LXXV, 827-828).
25. *Dialogues* IV. 36.
26. E. R. Curtius, *European Literature and the Latin Middle Ages*, p. 105.
27. *Dialogues* IV. 42.
28. *Ibid.*, IV. 43.
29. I do not distinguish between vision and dream here because it seems to me that Gregory does not so distinguish and that one might well include visions under the classifications of IV. 50.
30. Aelfric is among its critics; see *Catholic Homilies* II, p. 332 in the ed. of Benjamin Thorpe (Aelfric Society; London, 1846).
31. For a perceptive discussion of the application of some of the problems raised in this section to biblical criticism, see Helen Gardner, *The Limits of Literary Criticism: Reflections on the Interpretation of Poetry and Scripture* (Riddell Memorial Lectures; London: Oxford University Press, 1956).
32. The pertinent works are *Mimesis: The Representation of Reality in Western Literature,* trans. Willard Trask (Anchor Books; Garden City, N.Y.: Doubleday, 1957); "Figura," trans. Ralph Manheim in Auerbach's *Scenes from the Drama of European Literature: Six Essays* (New York: Meridian Books, 1959), pp. 11-76; and *Dante: Poet of the Secular World.*
33. *Mimesis,* p. 13.
34. For a recent study of the use of the Old Testament in the primitive church, see Barnabas Lindars, *New Testament Apologetic: The Doctrinal Significance of the Old Testament Quotations* (Philadelphia: Westminster Press, 1961).
35. Auerbach, "Figura," pp. 53-54. Used with permission.
36. *Ibid.*, p. 55.
37. Gregory of Tours, *History of the Franks,* II. 31; trans. O. M. Dalton (2 vols; Oxford: Clarendon Press, 1927).
38. "Figura," p. 58.
39. *Mimesis,* p. 136.
40. *Against Heresies* V. xiii. 3-4.
41. *Contra Celsum* V. 23.
42. *On the Resurrection of the Flesh* XIV.
43. See *Dialogues*, I. Preface.
44. See *Mimesis,* p. 279.

INDEX